The Martha Jackson Memorial Collection

The Martha Jackson Memorial Collection

HARRY RAND

Published for the

NATIONAL MUSEUM OF AMERICAN ART

by the

SMITHSONIAN INSTITUTION PRESS

WASHINGTON, D.C.

1985

Published on the occasion
of an exhibition organized by the
NATIONAL MUSEUM OF AMERICAN ART,
Smithsonian Institution, Washington, D.C.,
and shown there June 21–September 15, 1985

Curator for the exhibition: Harry Rand

Editor: Migs Grove

Library of Congress Catalogue Card No. 85-61684

PHOTO CREDITS

ALBRIGHT-KNOX ART GALLERY, Buffalo, New York, fig. 19

GEOFFREY CLEMENTS, Staten Island, New York, figs. 20, 34

STANLEY EDWARDS, Chicago, Illinois, fig. 28

HIRSHHORN MUSEUM AND SCULPTURE GARDEN, Smithsonian Institution,
    Washington, D.C., fig. 13

FRED W. MCDARRAH, New York, New York, fig. 37

THE METROPOLITAN MUSEUM OF ART, New York, New York, fig. 43

All other photographs were taken by the staff of the
NATIONAL MUSEUM OF AMERICAN ART, Smithsonian Institution,
Washington, D.C.

Cover: Norman Bluhm, detail of *Acheron* (cat. no 4)

Contents

Foreword

CHARLES C. ELDREDGE
Director

Martha Kellogg Jackson never intended to form an art collection in the usual sense. She did not, for instance, identify a single style or period or medium and then search for examples to complete a survey of the subject. Neither did she assemble disparate artworks solely for her idiosyncratic delight, without regard for consideration or appreciation of others. Rather, she acquired artists for the Martha Jackson Gallery and, as evidence of her good faith in offering their works for public sale, she selected similar artworks to keep for herself. She collected intuitively, without a predetermined idea of how the collection would ultimately develop, trusting in her taste and temperment to unify the choices. So, she was able to embrace the diverse currents of art in the 1950s and 1960s, ranging from the figurative to the abstract, the impassioned to the serene, the heroic, and the subtle. The collection in its catholicity suggests something of the breadth of understanding and enthusiasm that Martha Jackson brought to her calling as an art dealer and retrospectively surveys the activities of an important gallery in an important era. Framed not by the telescoping lens of history but by the wide-angle lens of contemporary experience, the collection provides a special view of a fecund epoch and a barometer of taste for one of its key players.

Illustrated by those works (and artists) she held particularly dear—in a number of cases, examples of singular accomplishment and impact—this exhibition and catalogue are, then, a kind of album of Jackson's professional life. And what a remarkable life it was! In retrospect one is aware of its adventuresome spirit and feminist overtones: inspired by Adelyn Dohme Breeskin, the young Jackson committed herself to art and chose career over marriage at a time when one often precluded the other. In her career, she championed an unusual number of women artists, among them Louise Nevelson, Grace Hartigan, Marisol, Joan Mitchell, Chryssa, and Claire Falkenstein. She also brought equality of opportunity to the closed society of the New York art world, featuring the work of such talented minority artists as Eldzier Cortor, Bob Thompson, and Emilio Cruz. Well-established artists and Martha Jackson's "discoveries" alike speak fondly of her personal warmth and her loyalty.

Her legacy is documented in the Martha Jackson Memorial Collection, which was generously donated to the National Museum of American Art by her son and successor at the gallery, David Anderson. His benefaction (which included a simultaneous gift of her European works to the Smithsonian's Hirshhorn Museum) will help subsequent generations trace within the national collections the many branchings and graftings of this fertile period of modern art, and to him we are all indebted for his thoughtful donations.

To the many artists and friends of Martha Jackson who offered their recollections of her and the gallery, my thanks for their gracious cooperation. I am grateful as well to Harry Rand, curator in the museum's Department of Painting and Sculpture, for his care and diligence in weaving those memories and his own insights into an informative catalogue essay. The efforts of many museum colleagues were required to prepare the exhibition and catalogue, and I greatly appreciate the excellent work of all those who contributed to the venture. As always, the professional expertise of the Smithsonian Institution Press ensured the high quality of the catalogue design and production.

The Martha Jackson Memorial Collection

HARRY RAND

Martha Kellogg (Jackson) was born in Buffalo, New York, in 1907 to Cyrena Allen Case and Howard Kellogg. Her socially prominent family owned the Kellogg Chemical Company and, over a period of several generations, included executive engineers of aviation instruments, while the family's business was manufacturing vegetable oils. Martha Kellogg Jackson never thought of herself as descending from an artistic lineage, although her grandmother—the niece of Elihu Vedder—was a painter. Martha's uncle, Spencer Kellogg, Jr., was one of the first natives of Buffalo to recognize the talent of Charles Burchfield, who practiced his art obscurely in that community. Another uncle, Donald Kellogg, had a collection famous for four major Rufino Tamayo paintings. Both uncles lived in Paris after the war and, as Martha Jackson recalled, "never had the sense to buy Picasso or Matisse."

Martha attended the Park School in Buffalo and was an accomplished rider who showed the family's celebrated stable of horses. As an adult she still limped noticeably—the result of a childhood riding accident that stiffened one leg, which never seemed to slow her down or dampen her high spirits. Her love of horses played a diminishing role in her adult life. Yet, occasionally, this interest surfaced, as when she acquired Thomas Scott's *Portrait of Lexington* (cat. no. 114). Lexington was one of the foundation sires from which all other American thoroughbreds descend.

Although her family preferred an athletic life and healthy pursuits like riding, Martha Jackson studied as much literature as she could. This pleased her family, who would have condoned her becoming a writer; she majored in English when she attended Smith College from 1925 to 1928.

A supporter of the Albright Art Gallery (now the Albright-Knox Art Gallery) when Andrew Ritchie was the director in the 1940s, Martha Jackson was elected to the Members' Advisory Council in 1944. She assumed the directorship of the Art Committee of the Garret Club and strongly influenced Buffalo's taste and collecting, yet only when she moved from her native city did the potential of her artistic interest begin to appear. Martha Jackson began her study of art history in Baltimore. She enrolled in a course at the Baltimore Museum of Art and Johns Hopkins University and fell under the sway of the first powerful art historian she was to know. A model for three generations of art professionals, Adelyn Dohme Breeskin recalled Jackson as

...a very quiet, rather shy young woman [who] came to see me in my office at the Baltimore Museum of Art. She ...asked if I thought she would be eligible to take [my] course [on modern art] when she not only knew nothing about art but had never heard about it in her home. I told her that she could certainly join the class and would probably have less to unlearn under the circumstances she had mentioned. Indeed, she proved a very apt pupil and before long approached me about purchasing a painting by Marc Chagall which we had for sale in our one-man show at our museum. She chose an especially handsome work and shortly after that...the Museum of Modern Art...exhibited [it]. It was shortly after that she launched her New York gallery and was on her way to becoming one of the ablest gallery owners as well as a most astute collector of art.[1]

In 1949 Martha Jackson moved to New York where she studied at the Museum of Modern Art and the Hans Hofmann School of Art. It was in New York that the full implications of her interest took shape. Her son and future gallery colleague, David Anderson, recalls the odd turn of events that followed.

I have always wondered what the future might have been had my stepfather shown some enthusiasm for the

1

Chagall.…Dave Jackson called it "that damned fried egg of Martha's" in response to its particularly prominent, radiant sun, and Martha's innate instincts were deflected (temporarily) to collecting furniture and Staffordshire.

Of course it was other more serious differences that resulted, in 1949, in divorce and Martha's move to New York. Later, Martha credited her years with David Jackson (a lawyer whose thought processes marched with military discipline) as a great help to her in business, and felt it fitting (if also ironic) that her Gallery and Collection bear his name.

It was in New York that her walls really blossomed— Bill de Kooning's Night Square, Marin's Circus, the early Hofmann Afterglow and others. Now, her new acquisitions represented the visible evidences of Martha's instinct for personal discoveries and enthusiasms rather than a collection shaped by an overview of knowledge.… These acquisitions also marked the route of a deepening involvement. Not satisfied just to buy their work, Martha also had to meet and get to know the artists. It was Hans Hofmann who first suggested the idea of opening a gallery.

It was an unforgettable shock to see, on a visit up from school, the small dark room in the back of the new gallery on East 66th Street that replaced Martha's sunny Eastside [sic] apartment. Nothing was spared in the excitement and enthusiasm of her effort to launch this new venture (including my Sunday off, spent filling and stamping envelopes).…It is impossible for me not to think of the many formidable works acquired like the Chagall only to depart again later, sacrificed to assist the growth of the Gallery and the accumulation of works by the artists represented.

Dynamics played an important part in acquisitions too. More than once Martha told me, "If you are going to buy something, it's a good idea to buy two: one to keep and one to sell." She was a frequent visitor to artist's studios, galleries and museums, and rarely returned from a trip without some newly purchased works ("to help pay the expenses"). And of course, she would buy work from artists she liked but didn't represent if they needed the money.[2]

Between 1949 and 1953 Martha Jackson continued to collect and on March 24, 1953, she opened a gallery in a converted brownstone house at 22 East 66th Street. In a press release issued at that time Martha Jackson stated her interests and ambitions for the gallery.

I feel there should be a larger market for paintings by American artists.…I believe there is a great potential out-of-town market for such paintings. But the out-of-towner who wants to start his own collection is often either timid or bewildered when he comes to New York to make his first selection. There is no small informal place where he can see a varied group of artists, styles and periods.… The Martha Jackson Gallery will be a very informal place where the new collector can come in and express his preferences without feeling he is committing lèse majesté toward artists who may be especially sponsored by the gallery visited. I intend to show all media: oil, watercolor, graphic art, etc. European artists will not be ruled out but my emphasis will be on Americans.[3]

Her position was not that of a teacher or a patron but that usually suspect role of a dealer with commercial interests. To her this financial aspect was the least important component of her operation. One of those to benefit from her taste and leadership and, in turn, become one of the towering figures in American art, Seymour H. Knox, recalled his enthusiasm for Martha Jackson's burgeoning involvement with the visual arts.

It is not an easy task for anyone to open an art gallery in New York and compete with the many other dealers already established there. As a friend of Martha Jackson and a fellow Buffalonian, I was most interested in the progress of her venture. Frequent visits to the Martha Jackson Gallery impressed me with the quality of her collection, the variety of the artists she represented and, especially, her enthusiasm for and belief in contemporary art.

Her taste in the selection of her collection and confidence in the artists in her gallery has since been justified. Throughout the years she was most helpful to me with her encouragement to continue to collect art of the present.[4]

On another occasion Knox was more magnanimous and described how Martha Jackson's taste assisted him in shaping one of the foremost collections of modern art. Her indirect, if decisive, effect on these holdings helped form the very terms by which we view recent art history:

It was through her that I became largely interested in paintings. That was before she opened her gallery in New York in the late '40s. From the beginning the Albright-Knox and Martha Jackson had a strong relationship, and a number of the most outstanding works in our collection were purchased through her gallery and still are. Through Martha I met the artists who were to become prominent in the early '50s—Karel Appel, Sam Francis, John Hultberg, Michael Goldberg, the Spanish artist Tapies—all artists she represented, all now in our collection.[5]

Eldzier Cortor, virtually an unknown black Chicago painter who had lived in Cuba, Haiti, and Mexico, was among the first artists represented by the gallery. Born in Richmond, Virginia, he studied at the Art Institute of Chicago and taught at the Centre D'Art, Port-au-Prince; he has held numerous awards and fellowships and has exhibited widely. In particular he painted the lithe and handsome Gullah Negroes, natives of the Sea Islands off the coast of South Carolina. Elongated females, poised as ebony ballerinas, are a major theme in his work; *Southern Gate* (fig. 1) is certainly the most celebrated example.

Exhibited in numerous shows, it was illustrated in a full-page color reproduction in *Life* Magazine (July 1946). It belongs to a series of paintings that treated the South, which Cortor recalls

…extended over a number of years starting with my travels to the Sea Islands of coastal South Carolina and Georgia on a Rosenwald Fellowship, making portrayals of Sea Island people of African heritage.

Figure 1. Eldzier Cortor, *Southern Gate*, 1942–43 (cat. no. 23)

In the creating of the painting Southern Gate *much is owed to a 1941 exhibit titled "Masterpieces of French Art" that, due to the vicissitudes of war, was touring this country. The large show contained original works that had never left their walls before from the Louvre Museum and French state museums. I was greatly impressed by the painters of the Romantic movement in the exhibit, Delacroix being the uppermost influence at the time. Also, at the time, I attended some lecture on the application of paint materials and methods given by Jacques Maroger, a former Louvre Museum conservator, then residing in this country.*

Southern Gate was purchased in 1944 from the traveling exhibition "New Names in American Art" then being shown at the Baltimore Museum of Art. At the time I did not know who bought the painting. It was not until about nine years later that...a good friend...at the Art Institute of Chicago, made mention of a recent visit to the Art Institute of a lady who owned a painting of mine and who had just opened a gallery in New York. Since I was in New York looking for a gallery he suggested that I should get in touch with her. Naturally, later on, I was both surprised and delighted to find out it was Martha Jackson....I feel the painting was apparently a rather personal painting to her since it was always on a wall in her living quarters when it was not on exhibit over the years.[6]

When he exhibited his work in Washington, D.C., the *Washington Star* observed that Cortor's "craftsmanship is outstanding,"[7] while the *Washington Post* thought his works' "greatest weakness is a too fluent illustrational tendency."[8] The languor of his painting might prove too heady for some, but, for those who enter the dream world of the steamy deep South and the freedom of the Sea Islands, the intoxication is complete.

Cortor's relations with the gallery were mutually beneficial, and the artist discovered, as others would over the years, that Martha Jackson's taste was broad, not limited by doctrinaire considerations.

The wide range of styles covered by the gallery was apparent. Martha Jackson was not one of limited taste; also, her balancing of the known and the lesser known artists together in exhibition—I found both of these qualities to be admired. In the early days of the gallery I sometimes helped Martha with some of her framing and hanging for exhibitions. During these times I found her to have a great sense of humor, and also to be a marvelous teller of artist stories.[9]

Almost from the time the gallery opened, Martha Jackson became associated with the New York School. Referred to as the "intra-subjectives" early on, these artists were sometimes called "action painters," or "abstract expressionists," and later they were known as practitioners of "painterly abstraction." Each critical camp had its own title for this loose artistic fellowship and from each viewpoint this efflorescence of postwar art seemed the harbinger of some other direction in modern art. Sometimes the designations were derisive; other names for these artists sought to enlist their support of a historical reading of their sources and goals, but, finally, the more-or-less neutral term New York School came to stand for the entire movement. The events that brought this movement into being and maintained it in the public's awareness took place mainly in New York, even though few of the artists in the movement actually came from New York. Like Martha Jackson herself, circumstance and a desire to engage seriously in the pursuit of some aspect of modern art brought a legion of talented personalities to the city.

Figure 2. James Brooks, *Harmagh*, 1967 (cat. no. 9)

One of the first artists associated with the gallery was James Brooks, a member of the "first generation" of the New York School and an artist whose reputation has grown with every passing year. Harold Rosenberg sketched Brooks's position among his contemporaries:

> He lacked the crisis personality of Pollock, de Kooning, or Kline, the exuberance of Hofmann, the nervous self-questioning of Guston. Brooks showed no sign of being attracted to the metaphysical postulates of Action Painting or to its aims of penetrating reality or changing the artist's self.[10]

This assessment of Brooks's work bespeaks the critic's notion that such modern painting was capable of penetrating reality by retrieving those psychological experiences acquired during the development of the artist's personality. His sentiment was echoed by others who noted that Brooks's paintings were admired for a

> ...sensuous beauty, a formal control and an orchestrated color which are not the common products of pure spontaneity or introspection. If he is indeed an abstract expressionist, he is probably the most ingratiating one....[11]

Despite his reputation for grace rather than rebellion, thoughtful evolution rather than compulsion, Brooks was a member of The Irascible Eighteen. This term first appeared in a May 1950 *New York Herald Tribune* editorial, which referred to a group of artists who refused to submit their works to a national juried exhibition, *American Painting Today: 1950*, at the Metropolitan Museum of Art. In fact, a staunchly ethical and somewhat reticent artist, the soft-spoken Brooks had a substantial career behind him even then. Under the Federal Art Project he had been a muralist with affinities to the regionalists, although he neither countenanced the regionalists' provincialism nor shared their repudiation

4

of European modernism. His art evolved toward abstraction during the four-year period he worked on a set of huge murals for LaGuardia Airport in New York. In reaction to the careful style he developed for those murals, Irving Sandler noted, "after 1948, he began to paint more directly and freely, his canvases growing looser, more fragmented and abstract."[12]

That tendency in his work eventually produced such lovely paintings as *Harmagh* (fig. 2), a picture that Brooks himself held in the highest regard.[13] It seems to be named for the county and county seat of Armagh in the southern part of Northern Ireland. Its deep cool colors invite the spectator to enter a midnight realm of visual wandering, its forms recalling landscape and seascape. When this work was shown as part of Martha Jackson's collection in the mid-1970s it was singled out for praise. Joseph Masheck observed the diminution of recent art by the dross of accumulated criticism.

> *Some of the American painters...have been reduced to small potatoes...and succeeding masters and styles appear in these hospitable circumstances to be more worthwhile than we knew. Joan Mitchell's* Untitled, 1959, *is a case in point...James Brooks'* Harmagh, *from 1967, succeeds in fanning the old embers.*[14]

Indeed, revisionist history and a revived taste for abstract expressionism, as well as a new appreciation of Brooks's painting, has rectified the situation that held true at the time of this review. The tide upon which the taste for abstract art at first went out, then returned, was one that Martha Jackson did not live to see through its full cycle. Never in her lifetime did the gallery's association with the style come under serious attack, and she never had to fend off fundamentally unsympathetic criticism that measured this art from a wholly alien viewpoint.

Brooks's recollections of his association with Martha Jackson are vivid:

> *I rarely heard Martha Jackson's rather flat, nasal voice raised on any subject but art, by which she was obsessed; but it was heard often on that....*
>
> *My wife Charlotte (and I) had met her in East Hampton when she had become curious about artists who had settled in her vicinity, and we came to know her better when she was guided to our remote cottage and studio-barn in Montauk overlooking Long Island Sound by Elaine de Kooning. She was bringing the English painter William Scott, whose work she showed at her New York gallery.... We would see her afterward sporadically—several times with Karel Appel, the painter of the Cobra group— her gallery by then had a slightly international cast. That was in 1953....*
>
> *I joined her gallery in 1967. It occupied the whole of a fine building on East Sixty-Ninth Street just east of Madison Avenue. It had an unusually designed interior; was well, perhaps overstaffed with the most agreeable people I could imagine, and it was a great pleasure to visit them there.*[15]

Figure 3. James Brooks, *Oran*, 1969 (cat. no. 10)

In contrast to the dark complexity of *Harmagh's* swirling surface, *Oran* (fig. 3) is a bright, light-filled work of a few, large shapes. These simply defined forms are legible in a way that the previous, perhaps more painterly, pieces were not. Compared to the flowing liquid forms that interpenetrate one another in *Harmagh*, the edges of shapes in *Oran* lock while the higher valued colors propose a quiet contemplation of nature. Emphasizing the viscous property of the paint itself—its physical substance rather than optical character as pure hue— Brooks encouraged selected incidents to develop in his work. As quiescent, lyrical, and rational as his pictures appear, his approach depends on the "controlled accident" at the heart of dada and surrealism. In this, his painting showed a slow, progressive, and consistent evolution beginning in the late 1940s. Brooks worked without dramatic deviation in his approach, which he has kept in controlled experimentation over decades.

As Brooks noted, Martha Jackson embraced much more than the fine arts of the United States. When she decided to show a European émigré she chose the expressionist architect Frederick Kiesler. Lillian Kiesler, widow of the great visionary architect and theoretician, recalls Kiesler's meeting and the subsequent deliberations.

> *During the last year of his life she approached him to join her gallery. I can remember her first discussion in East Hampton—and Frederick listening with a bemused attitude.*

Later, much later, just as he was actually joining (that is, she was making attractive financial offers) he said, "Here is Martha with her wilted blond hair, an atmosphere of a loser, a victim, a deep sadness in her, certainly not a woman with charisma—that which arouses enthusiasm—her gallery a nightmare, mostly windows—yet, she has a deepness of purpose, she really wants me in her gallery, and backs it up with action, more than others; therefore I am moved and will join the gallery.[16]

The insight that prompted her to include Kiesler in her gallery of mostly irreverent young experimenters permeated all that she did and may have constituted—more than any business acumen or art historical insight—her greatest talent. Amy Baker Sandback explains that

Martha is an important figure because she had the energy to shape a different kind of world for herself. She was straightforward and never made excuses. She acted on what she thought. And sometimes I think that her quality of stubbornness was her genius and I know that was her charm.[17]

If Martha Jackson had a proclivity for the slightly exotic—the European, the Japanese, or Mexican, the experimental and questioning artists among the modern Americans—she united all these without regard for considerations other than quality and her stubborn integrity. For a Christmas show in December 1953 she gathered a diverse group of artists, including the unknown Gandy Brody and the celebrated Reginald Marsh, the Canadian Alexander Luke and the Spanish surrealist Antoni Tapies; best of all, the works were priced under $100. According to one reviewer, the paintings included

about a half dozen which make us forget these larger questions for sheer enjoyment. Childe Hassam's 1907 Beach at Bass Rocks, *a mosiac-like watercolor of irregular pieces beautifully fitted,* Marin's circus picture In the Ring, *and Prendergast's* Blue Water, *a solid, rhythmical composed group of figures are outstanding.*[18]

Gandy Brody enjoyed a paradoxically high professional recognition during his life, but relatively little public appreciation. Born in New York, Brody was inspired to paint after he saw Van Gogh's *Starry Night* and the Klees and Picassos at the Museum of Modern Art. He traveled and studied in Mexico, France, Italy, and Spain and was a pupil of Hans Hofmann, Martha Graham, Meyer Schapiro, and Lionello Venturi. His paintings were acquired by the Metropolitan Museum of Art, the Whitney Museum of American Art, the Phillips Collection, the Baltimore Museum of Art, the Chrysler Museum, the Hirshhorn Museum and Sculpture Garden, the Museum of Modern Art and other estimable collections, yet few in the general population knew his expressionist works. One of his pieces, *A Chivalrous Knight* (fig. 4), epitomizes what Ethel Schwabacher referred to when she described his work of that year, noting:

He has elevated the child's world to expression in terms of a highly developed artistry. He retains the primitive depth of sensory experience. It underlies his work—but he presents it with the skill of a mature craftsman....Gandy is now in the position to show how young painters of unusual ability may profit from the revolutionary inheritances of a score of 20th-century painters from Mondrian to Gorky, given great sensitivity, tenacity, and an imperviousness to the lure of quick success.[19]

Sadly, this promise was cut short by Brody's early death, and what remains are his haunting images recalling childhood and primitive civilizations. Meyer Schapiro remarked on the unusually captivating quality of Brody's work.

We see through his pictures that the familiar world has not lost its spell for the artist. It is still a sphere of revelation and mystery and we are drawn into it more deeply by Gandy's beautiful paintings.[20]

Finally, Brody's cosmopolitanism encouraged him to trespass the bounds of usual "good taste" and his confidence was sufficiently visible to other artists. At a memorial service the sculptor Isaak Witkin summarized the feelings of many who knew Brody:

Gandy's vision of art was in opposition to the concept of modernism in all its superficial manifestations. This is not to say, however, that he was a reactionary or that he hated modern art. On the contrary, he loved the art of this century more than any other. He reacted to the narrow concept of Art History that did not embrace the whole panorama of artistic experience from Paleolithic art to Mondrian and Pollock....[21]

Brody's career was meteoric, resembling none other of his time, although Martha Jackson never had a contractual relationship with him. In the Martha Jackson Memorial Collection his work holds a special place, for his lot was not that of the typical artist supported by the gallery.

Many of the young Americans that exhibited at the Martha Jackson Gallery had a common background—military service followed by study in Europe. A West Coast artist Lawrence Calcagno served in the Army Air Corps between 1941 and 1945, during which time he won a major prize in the Army Arts Contest at the National Gallery, Washington, D.C. Upon his discharge, he painted and traveled in Mexico until 1947 when he returned to train at the California School of Fine Arts in San Francisco. Under the GI Bill of Rights he studied at the Académie Grande Chaumière in Paris and the Academia delgi Belli Arte in Florence, after which he spent six months in Morocco and North Africa. He came to the attention of New York dealers only after his return from Europe.

In December 1953 he stopped in New York to see

Figure 4. Gandy Brody, *A Chivalrous Knight*, 1954 (cat. no. 8)

friends on his way back to California; Clyfford Still, his teacher in San Francisco, introduced him to Dorothy Miller who invited Calcagno to leave some of his work at her office in the Museum of Modern Art so that he would have a place to bring dealers. Martha Jackson was invited to view his work and impressed Calcagno as someone who wanted to raise the quality and recognition of American arts to the level of the international art scene. She asked Calcagno to participate in the gallery's 1954 exhibition, *New Talent*. She succeeded in selling some of his works when the young painter told her that he

> wanted to return to Paris for another year, where I had already been exhibiting work at Paul Facchetti's Gallery (who had shown the first Jackson Pollocks in Paris in 1952). She offered to subsidize me in Paris for a year. A month later, in May of 1954, she came to Europe. She was eager to develop an international connection with a modern gallery in Paris. I introduced her to Paul Facchetti....she was struck by the work of Karel Appel....she purchased his work later at the Venice Biennale where he

> was showing at the Dutch Pavilion. I introduced Martha to most of the American artists I knew working in Paris at that time. She purchased works from and subsidized the painters: John Hultberg, Sam Francis and myself, who were living in Paris, and scheduled exhibitions of our work in her New York gallery. She later showed in New York the works of Norman Bluhm and Paul Jenkins who had met her in Paris at that time.[22]

David Anderson joined his mother in Paris to view the art and to celebrate his birthday. They cruised the North Sea before returning to Paris where Jackson invited Hultberg, Francis, and Calcagno to accompany her to the Venice Biennale; she paid for their train tickets.

> We left Paris together on the night train, the Orient Express, Martha in the first-class Pullman section and we three in the rear, third-class section. We had brought bread, cheese and a jug of red wine, and enjoyed a merry and exciting time, anticipating the Biennale and Venice. The painters Norman Bluhm and Paul Jenkins had joined us at the railroad station, inviting themselves along....It was an exciting time for all of us and we poor starving

Figure 5. Lawrence Calcagno, *Night at Mattoon,* 1959 (cat. no. 20)

artists had much enjoyment in the company of Martha Jackson, who in our eyes was our rich patroness from the U.S. and, at the same time, an impressive and serious art dealer.[23]

In fact, by that time Jackson had already been associated with Hans Hofmann, Jackson Pollock, James Brooks, and Willem de Kooning, so that she was becoming quite prominent. To her youthful protégés (as to many other observers) her wealth may have appeared greater than it was; she had an annual income from trust funds of between $10,000 and $12,000, which was then a considerable sum—although not of sufficient magnitude to meet the needs both of the gallery and an indulgent style of living. In general she had to forgo the pleasures of the very rich. Instead, the gallery became a discipline that governed the pattern of her life. She scrimped to meet her economic needs and raised funds for the gallery by selling much of the family furniture and silver, as well as some paintings she owned. Even though she would not

have been destitute had the gallery failed, it was a matter of economic necessity that it succeed. She never revealed this urgency to her artists, for, patrician by upbringing, Martha Jackson was rarely the casual confessor and displayed a reserve in affairs concerning self-sufficiency.

Her gallery quickly gained a solid reputation in Europe because she bought "difficult" abstract artists from the European dealers in addition to advertising her exhibitions in the European art magazines. Calcagno was the beneficiary of these European connections:

In early August, I returned to Spain, to Barcelona, to have the little catalogue printed of my forthcoming first one-man show in Martha's New York gallery which was scheduled to take place in September, when I returned to the U.S. Martha arranged for me to stay with Antoni Tapies and his wife in their apartment in Barcelona. He took me to a good printer who printed the catalogue for an extremely reasonable price and shipped it to Martha in New York. Martha's objective in all this was economy....[24]

8

Notices of the September exhibition were generally considerate and sympathetic. One reviewer proposed,

His abstractions are vision-suggestive.... They are landscapes: the reflections of hills and skies in lakes; down-crashing surfs; solitudes crossed by waves of purple and magenta (or by other equally startling colors)...the color is striking. Stretch the imagination and one may detect a thread tying him to the more violent Clyfford Still with whom he at one time studied....[25]

A work of this period, *Night Tide, XVII* (cat. no. 19), documents the introduction of his mature work to New York. A later piece, *Night at Mattoon* (fig. 5), is a far more lyrical and appealing picture, displaying a thickly painted dark field of heavily textured pigment that is broken by five swirling patches of murky, unlit colors laced with white and bordered with a wide blue band along the left side. His work met with the most diverse critical reception: some, like the English critic Bryan Robertson, applauded the work; others expressed considerably less enthusiasm.[26]

Eventually, Calcagno and Martha Jackson had a falling-out; Calcagno went his way to develop his art. Recalling the days of his association with the gallery the artist remembers,

The attitude of artists and dealers have changed a lot since then. In a way, Martha was correct when she warned that I would risk my career if I left her gallery. However, professional fame and fortune were not the primary objectives of my life as an artist....I felt uncomfortable and at a great disadvantage in the limelight. Although I have dealt with many dealers since, none has been so admirable and meaningful to me. I continue to paint and prosper modestly, and I am indeed free. This has been my measure of success. Yet, during these many years, Martha Jackson continues as the cornerstone in my life and career. I continue to admire and pay tribute to her memory.[27]

Perhaps the artist who, more than any other, was intimately associated with the gallery for many years is John Hultberg. Born in Berkeley, California, he attended Fresno College (B.A., 1943) and returned to California after World War II. Although he participated in exhibitions at the California Palace of the Legion of Honor and elsewhere throughout the country, his work was still mainly visible in the Bay Area. Between 1949 and 1951 he studied at the Art Students League in New York; his first solo exhibition was in 1952 at the Korman Gallery. In 1954 Hultberg moved to Paris, and the next year won the first prize in oil painting at the Corcoran Biennial; his second one-man show was held in 1955 at the Martha Jackson Gallery.

A work from that period is the mysterious *Imaginary Landscape* (fig. 6), whose delicate surface treatment and wide range of values hinted at the illegible forms and terrain that would come into focus in Hultberg's later

Figure 6. John Hultberg, *Imaginary Landscape,* 1954 (cat. no. 49)

pieces. Incidental passages indicate some sort of technology amid biomorphic nature that, receding into a deep space, recalls Gorky's black paintings of the middle 1940s. More than Hultberg's choice of materials—deep inky washes on paper—accounted for his shapes' relatively soft contours at this time. For example, the composition's dramatic left edge suspends a lightly waving opaque border that moves up the paper separating the white of the background from the other shapes that describe a deep space akin to landscapes.

Hultberg's work developed in a pattern atypical of his generation's discovery of its reservoir of images. In an unusual evolution, Hultberg reached his overt subject matter over the years. As time passed, the solid forms of his figures and shapes emerged from their mere approximations—as if a fog were progressively lifting from a nightmarish scene that he was recording over and over again. He seems to have been continually finding the courage to name, ever more specifically, the tragic things toward which he was groping. In this pattern of self-discovery he markedly differed from his contemporaries whose subject matter, once named, underwent a formal analysis that dissolved shapes into even less recognizable patterns.

In the early years of his career, Hultberg's honors and achievements continued to accrue at the same satisfyingly rapid pace as his first acclamation; invitations and awards came from all over the world for an art that was (and is) highly idiosyncratic and that provoked divergent reactions whenever it was shown. The work has been noted and chronicled as not quite comprehensible but obviously eloquent; it has seemed to many a troubling and intelligent expression of this century's middle years.

Figure 7. John Hultberg, *Machine Shop* (Showing Gantry Cranes, Newport News Shipyard), 1957 (cat. no. 52)

Figure 8. John Hultberg, *New City*, 1957 (cat. no. 53)

10

A typical work of the middle 1950s, *Imaginary Landscape* contained the elements of Hultberg's greatest strengths as well as liabilities. From the very first his work was deemed genuinely disturbing, yet it seemed potentially exhaustible—a horizon of depleted ideas that Hultberg himself has yet to cross. Writing in 1955 one reviewer observed that, "He has skill and a personal vision; both need refinement if he is to go beyond the striking impression he now makes. His work carries in it the seeds of repetition and self-indulgence."[28]

But such a view was certainly not universal, for the artist's appeal has been widespread. He received invitations to chronicle the industrial landscape of America and, in works like *Machine Shop* (fig. 7), he recorded an accurate image of the vast machinery of the world of factories. These images seemed to confirm for him the characteristics toward which he had been moving as the constituents of his subject matter.

Rather than being stymied by the repeated elements of Hultberg's paintings, Robert Rosenblum admired an appealing diversity of form: "All his works, however, are arresting, not only in the impact of their disquieting imagery, but in their intricate and fascinating manipulations of shapes and space."[29] In the relatively illegible *New City* (fig. 8)—with its three vanishing points of converging perspective and exaggerated feeling of depth from an elevated point of view—or in a work of the same year, *The Black Flag* (fig. 9), a hauntingly prescient statement was apparent to all viewers. His gripping and thoroughly novel subject matter separated him from his contemporaries and made him the legitimate ancestor of a type of visual imagery that became widespread, via science fiction movies, a generation later. That world becomes accessible whenever Hultberg

> opens his windows a little wider upon the lair of murder and mystery to which he makes his return in every painting and from which he escapes to the next....He is a one-subject painter. But it is a big subject.[30]

That threatening world quoted just enough of the world we inhabit to convince us of its prophetic possibility and to haunt us with the insistent quality of true nightmare—absolute conviction in the menacing illusion that we behold. Something of that ungraspable vision, a *fata morgana* that vanishes upon close inspection, occurs in *Blue Black Destruction* (fig. 10). The high value mass of the canvas presents several boxes that—resembling Dali's experiments with adjacent worlds, or Adolph Gottlieb's early experiments with partitioned symbols—admit vision to a different dimension. Some of the boxes appear to present cityscapes, others are aquatic; a catastrophic structural collapse is pictured in one, while a tree trunk is visible in yet another. Together a synthetic vision of accumulated gestures begins to mount as a newspaper from another time or world describes the partial and fragmentary events to an

Figure 9. John Hultberg, *The Black Flag*, 1957 (cat. no. 54)

Figure 10. John Hultberg, *Blue Black Destruction*, 1958 (cat. no. 55)

outsider—yet in Hultberg's world we are only partially strangers. John Ashberry commented on the mix of imagination and reality brought to Hultberg's task when he wrote that "color and the human from only point up further the inhumanity of his half-abstract, half-concrete universe."[31] Into the depiction of these partial machines and landscapes, Hultberg inserted characterless people, ciphers for human beings who perform some unknown and threatening work, and who also lend scale to shapes that would have been illegible otherwise. Our ignorance of what is actually transpiring in these pictures creates an emotional void into which we plunge as we speculate about human relationships within the work. "There is a sense of pervasive stillness," James Mellow wrote,

> a sense of being becalmed. The nearest equivalent that I can suggest is one of those moments when the humming of a motor, or the ticking of a clock—to which you have not been listening—stops abruptly and you are aware that something has gone wrong.[32]

Stillness and anticipation suffuse these works, as in a de Chirico where the quiet click and hum of electronics

Figure 11. John Hultberg, *Giant*, 1963 (cat. no. 62)

have been substituted for steam power. De Chirico's silently gliding, long-shadowed strollers and crepuscular statues have been replaced by equally mute technocrats. Both artists accelerated perspective recession by acutely converging orthogonals to a vanishing point, thus "entrapping" the spectator's vision deep within the work's interior space. The principal effective component of both artists' paintings seems, regardless of other ostensible subject matter, to be a long drawn out sigh of nostalgia or fear. Such surrealist predecessors as Ernst's *Airplane Traps* or Tanguy's extraterrestrial deserts come to mind as well.

By 1963 the gallery had mounted a small retrospective for the still-young artist, and, once again, the reviewers found themselves ill at ease with his work.

> In describing his work one finds oneself writing around it. It is like being in a drive-in movie and suddenly becoming aware that the screen is being watched, not by people, but by cars.[33]

Giant (fig. 11), perhaps Hultberg's largest painting, recalls the titanic landscape compositions of Turner or the vast embrace of Altdorfer's history paintings in

which a maelstrom looms above the spectator. This vastly ambitious work fearfully summarizes history and gathers us into the figure of the onlooking giant who, light streaming from his figure, blocks our path into the painting's interior; thus challenged, the space that we occupy outside the picture feels very comfortable until we recognize that the threats in this picture are borrowed from reality. A profile, or surrogate for the viewer, appears in a "window" (lower right) above what seems a bottomless abyss.

As the decade advanced, his work became more threatening and gloomy. In May 1970 one critic observed that Hultberg's

> new paintings are like visions of the end of the world; not unlike his past work, but more pessimistic, more disquieting...all images become images of disaster, relics and ruins of some Sci-Fi Pompeii on the day of judgment.[34]

That Hultberg was looking *backward* into our future placed his work in a delicate critical position which put him in jeopardy of being dismissed as a fantasist or a raving apocalyptic; neither was true, for his vision was based on a knowledge of progress occurring in the most advanced factories. He had, early in his career, moved through factories to inventory the sorts of spaces in which industry was conducted; he had not judged what he saw, but recorded his impressions. The vocabulary by which his records were transmitted was highly refined and immediately accessible to many viewers. For example, in *Under Red Glass* (fig. 12) a thin slit of white in the far background indicates that an open space is beheld across a great interior distance. Nothing like this exists in Piranesi's world, yet both artists were portraying the scene of real power, the muscle that moves societies—one depicted the ruins of a bygone civilization, the other warned of future threats. Hultberg barely acknowledges the external world—a bird flies near the top of the picture to suggest that the environment which we behold is entirely enclosed in the red-tinted glass—for this world seems to be capable of an independent existence. What he portrays, from the very center of a humanistic viewpoint, are the fruits of an anti-humanism gone on rampage; nothing that he shows is ever fundamentally false—*fantasy* that ignores physical laws.

With the greatest irony, some of the early works that looked like pure fiction (and earned him descriptions such as the one that allied him with marginal Sci-fi) appear, today, to be accurate descriptions of modern workplaces. He has been consistently ahead of developments in our conventional understanding of interior and exterior space, and if his vision has been regularly unsettling, such reactions may not reflect the worth of his art as much as the dread with which we are entering the future.

Martha Jackson held forth on 66th Street until 1956 when she moved her gallery to 32 East 69th Street. The gallery specialized in contemporary American and European artists, and—as she had announced years before—the building included a print gallery, a sculpture court, and two floors devoted to monthly exhibitions and private shows.[35] Her verve accomplished more than could ever have been expected of one who came late to the arts. She was the first American art dealer to understand the potential of the Venice Biennale and to encourage others to attend. She presented the first exhibition of German paintings after World War II and the first exhibition of Arshile Gorky's early paintings.[36] The United States's first exhibition of pop art, *New Forms—New Media*, was held in her gallery.

She dealt, with equal fervor and interest, in young American artists and developing Europeans, but her ability to unify her collection and to find the exemplary object amid an artist's current production made her shows an unsuspected gauge of the times. Indeed, the evenness of her taste was noted years later when a reviewer of her collection observed that "some of the things seem a bit dated today, but practically everything is a good example of what the artist was doing at the

Figure 12. John Hultberg, *Under Red Glass*, 1974 (cat. no. 73)

time."[37] Even the European/American survey that she mounted in May and June 1954 provided an occasion for making comparisons, if—after the war and in the wake of American hegemony in the arts—there remained any basis for critical separation by geography. A critic noted that *Young American and European Painters* "produces no clear-cut differentiations between the two continents, as these artists of serious and maturing talents share a common esthetic outlook."[38] Undoubtedly, part of the similarity in shared outlook was simply Martha Jackson's taste.

The Martha Jackson Gallery gave the first New York solo shows to, among others, Karel Appel, Christo, Adolph Gottlieb, John Chamberlain, Jim Dine, Louise Nevelson, Sam Francis, Barbara Hepworth, Paul Jenkins, Julian Stanczak, and Antoni Tapies. The gallery helped introduce the work of Willem de Kooning; Jackson's exhibition of his complete second series *Women* (1954) was especially helpful. This exhibition followed a thematic show called *Woman*, September–October 1953, in which the gallery combined works in all mediums by artists as diverse as de Kooning (a painting called *She*), Childe Hassam (a large 1908 watercolor, *Riverbank*), Yasuo Kuniyoshi, Henry Moore (a sketch for a sculpture), Jules Pascin, Moise Kisling, Bernard Buffet, Marcel Gromaire, Max Beckmann, William Glackens, Elie Nadelman, and Eldzier Cortor (*Southern Gate*). In another exhibition that year the gallery exhibited a group of "distinguished contemporaries [that] offers an informed slant on some of the latest and most favorably regarded reputations."[39] It was in this show that de Kooning quietly unveiled the first of the multifigured compositions among his *Women* paintings, presenting his subject with a companion figure. Jackson also mounted the first exhibition of op art in this country.

Throughout her gallery career Martha Jackson understood the importance of fully documenting her artists' works—whatever the cost—and maintaining a thorough art library with librarian on the premises. She introduced the idea of photographing her artists at work

Figure 13. Bob Thompson, *Le Roi Jones and His Family*, 1946, oil on canvas, 36⅜ x 48½ in. (92.2 x 123.0 cm.). Hirshhorn Museum and Sculpture Garden, Smithsonian Institution, Washington, D.C.

which, if the notion seems tied to the ethos of abstract expressionism, is still fashionable. The catalogues issued by the Martha Jackson Gallery set a standard for thoroughness, and this support was not lost on the artists who quickly saw the value in having a lasting record of their exhibitions. She was the first art dealer to start her own film company, Red Parrot Films Ltd., named for her well-known and almost universally detested pet, the talkative parrot Chuckie. (*Ivory Knife*, a film about the work of Paul Jenkins, won top honors in the Venice Biennale.)

I [S. D. Edwards] remember those little elevator doors opening, and then a melding of shrieks, my fiance's, mine certainly, and the parrot's. All was spilled Scotch, green and yellow and red and furious motion!...Martha appeared, and somehow this bird of 20 pounds and 40 inch wing span was returned to its barred domicile, gentle as a sparrow, but with a gleaming yellow eye trained on a brash young interloper....Martha explained to us that the bird was a wonderful watchdog and was 80 years old![40]

Although known as a remarkable "woman dealer," in that last moment when such gender distinctions still held sway, she would have been a prominent figure in any age.[41] One reviewer flatly stated, "Jackson was one of the first influential female art dealers, and certainly the most open-minded and eclectic of any, man or woman."[42] Around her grew up a sympathetic salon of artists and their friends, writers about art, filmmakers, and poets—all thrived in the receptive and experimental climate of her gallery that was also her home.

In the mid-'50s my friend John Hultberg...took me [Richard Diebenkorn] on a visit to her apartment. She was enthusiastic and energetic and there were excellent pictures hanging. I met Adolph Gottlieb there that evening.... I had good positive feelings about her presence on the American art scene....She was good to, and gave financial assistance to, artists in whom she believed during their period of difficulty.[43]

Years after starting her gallery she still maintained those ideals she had declared when she first opened her doors:

You should not be afraid of dealers. Rely on them, take their advice. Choose art dealers deeply involved in art and discovering artists. Art dealers are in closer contact with the dedicated young artists, the prominent-artists-to-be, than any other official group. [44]

Rosalind Constable sketched a picture of the dealer at work.

Of all the New York art dealers of that time Martha was the most diligent, traveling all over the United States and the world in search of new talent. We sometimes went on scouting trips together. Many Sundays in New York I have panted up those interminable flights of dirty stairs that lead to the lofts of undiscovered geniuses....She would never allow the disability of a stiff knee...to limit her activities. [45]

Once she discovered an artist—even one as far afield as Julian Stanczak who lived in Cincinnati (like Jim Dine before him)—convenience and her peculiar mixture of generosity and business acumen moved her to try to gather her brood nearby. Stanczak recalls:

One thing Martha never understood about me, or forgave me for, was that I choose to live outside of New York. For my art I did not need to be there; for raising my family I preferred to be somewhere else, crowds of people bother me; and above all, I don't believe that in order to pursue one's excellence one has to live in New York. Spiritually I am always there, even if I am physically 500 miles removed. Martha thrived on action, and New York provided this. She wanted to live a very intense life. [46]

Because she bought the youthful works of many artists, her collection contained pieces that have yet to attain the high prices of other, more mature, works in the "signature" styles. Also, she acquired and showed pivotal pieces, transitional works that served as bridges from one period or style to another. But, when her collection was finally gathered and shown in a posthumous exhibition, the critics remarked on her perspicacity and diligence:

...an exceptionally sensitive and diverse collection. It is worth seeing because it contains works that are atypical but of developmental significance and, as well, because some of the works are so sympathetically selected that one may gain insight even into artists whose work ordinarily does not appeal. [47]

The combined confidence in the artistic maturity of American painting with the growing awareness of its significance in the world scene soon flooded New York with talent from around the country, and the Martha Jackson Gallery became one of the city's liveliest centers of artistic exchange. Many lasting and important acquaintances were made there; some even resulted in major artistic collaboration (fig. 13).

One evening I [Gilbert Sorrentino] went to an opening at the Martha Jackson Gallery and Roi [Leroi Jones, later known as Imamu Amiri Baraka] was there with his wife Hettie. And we met. And of course repaired to the Cedar [Bar] from the gallery and in the Cedar...it was one of those incredible situations—you just bumped into people. Dear Paul Blackburn, Dan Rice, a kind of constant interaction. [48]

One of the key works in the Martha Jackson Memorial Collection is a picture that integrates much of the world of painting and literature in New York in the late 1950s—Michael Goldberg's *Sardines* (fig. 14). The painting is probably well known to countless people who have never seen it. The piece has become enmeshed in the history of a certain legendary portion of the twentieth century, its culture, personalities, and irrepressible character. Although the picture has a respectable exhibition history and is one of the key works in the "second-generation" of abstract expressionists, it owes its fame to a poem by Frank O'Hara. [49]

WHY I AM NOT A PAINTER

I am not a painter, I am a poet.
Why? I think I would rather be
a painter, but I am not. Well,

for instance, Mike Goldberg
is starting a painting. I drop in.
"Sit down and have a drink" he
says. I drink; we drink. I look
up. "You have SARDINES in it."
"Yes, it needed something there."
"Oh." I go and the days go by
and I drop in again. The painting
is going on, and I go, and the days
go by. I drop in. The painting is
finished. "Where's SARDINES?"
All that's left is just
letters, "It was too much," Mike says.

But me? One day I am thinking of
a color: orange. I write a line
about orange. Pretty soon it is a
whole page of words, not lines.
Then another page. There should be
so much more, not of orange, of
words, of how terrible orange is
and life. Days go by. It is even in
prose, I am a real poet. My poem
is finished and I haven't mentioned
orange yet. It's twelve poems, I call
it ORANGES. And one day in a gallery
I see Mike's painting, called SARDINES.

O'Hara's description of the artist and poet laboring during a protracted period is testimony to a certain pace of work, a cadence dictated by the method of working. This sense of time, at once urgent and languid, full of incident, but protracted sometimes for weeks, was noted

Figure 14. Michael Goldberg, *Sardines*, 1955 (cat. no. 40)

by spectators who recorded Goldberg's approach to painting: "Goldberg works 'wet and wet' (two to three weeks) on a canvas. He usually has several going at once, he throws away or scrapes down a lot of them."[50] *Sardines* readily shows the deliberation that went into its making. Traces of the underlying writing ("Sardines" and "Exit") peek through the painting, initiating and then mimicking thin strokes of paint that are themselves repeated in strips of tape laid across the surface. Layer after layer has been adjusted and echoed; each new touch corresponds in some manner to what preceded it until the whole surface begins to quiver with internal references. The intensity of such a work—despite its "messy" appearance in traditional terms—finally creates a compositional tension as careful and thorough as a geometrically derived design might have been in either a representational or abstract work. A contemporary reviewer observed:

> *The basic brush stroke of the big action paintings…is about two yards long; and the "action" structure is usually given in half a dozen or so of these enormous strokes. …there is no discernible emotion in the work, nor anything so positive as gaiety, but there is a certain delicacy and prevailing cheer, and these qualities are enough to support the desire for loveliness.*[51]

The innovation that sustained such broad strokes was the increased size of the canvas, which had been extended and dilated by American artists during the 1940s. For its time *Sardines* was not a particularly big work, but when we view the rapid enlargement of the American easel painting during this period one is wonder struck at how, lacking any special architectural setting into which these paintings might be set, artist after artist produced such pictures. These, in their turn, would be dwarfed by gargantuan paintings which, if they seemed enormous at the time, now feel manageable and neither overblown nor in excess of the means required for their proper realization. Reviewers who concentrated on the choice of hue and palette instead of the energy of the brush stroke derived a very different impression from Goldberg's work. Some felt in these works the raw underside of urban despondency and violence. Tough, violent, resilient accommodation to a reality beyond the control of the individual, these paintings seemed to be treating a rude world that Goldberg invited us to see through paintings that

> *…become grimy windows that look inward—gestures of identity—and outward, reflecting the glare of nocturnal streets or of all-night greasy-spoons—seamy but warm. Goldberg is one of the most talented and knowledgeable young artists on the New York scene.*[52]

In fact, some of the work of this period, such as *The Creeks* (fig. 15), are coolly lyrical and use luscious pigment dominated by a rich blue.

Another of the stalwarts of the "second generation" of the New York School is Norman Bluhm, who is not

Figure 15. Michael Goldberg, *The Creeks*, 1959 (cat. no. 41)

always very pleased with that association. "'I'm known,' he growls ironically, 'as a goddam second-generation abstract expressionist.'"[53] Bluhm came to painting after growing up in Chicago; before he was seventeen he studied architecture with Mies van der Rohe. During World War II Bluhm was in the Army Air Corps; after the war he returned to the study of Mies's architecture before going to Paris, between 1947 and 1956 to paint. There he studied at the Ecole des Beaux-Arts and the Académie de la Grande Chaumiere. On his return he settled in New York and first exhibited at the Martha Jackson Gallery as part of a group show, *New Aspects of Space*, in the spring of 1957; the next autumn he had a solo exhibition at the Leo Castelli Gallery. Although Bluhm's formal study of painting was limited, he had been indoctrinated into the formal Bauhaus discipline of Mies, the precision and rigor of which is conspicuously missing from his work's appearance. Indeed, the casual viewer would be hard pressed to locate anything of the rational or geometric in Bluhm's explosively Dionysian works, paintings that apparently allow any excess of size, color, painthandling, and brushwork.

Bluhm is another of those robust painters (like Michael Goldberg or Grace Hartigan) who collaborated with Frank O'Hara. In one day in October 1960 Bluhm and O'Hara executed a series of *Poem Paintings*; this free-wheeling cooperative participation typified his work. A key to the character of Bluhm's painting can be found in a statement by Thomas Hess on the occasion of an exhibition at a gallery, operated by David Anderson and Jack Mayer, in Paris during the 1960s.

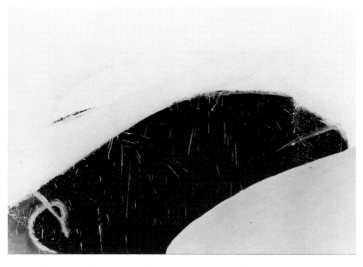

Figure 16. Norman Bluhm, *Acheron* (triptych), 1971 (cat. no. 4)

*One of the first things a pilot learns is to think of his air-
plane as a motionless object with a river of air streaming
past it. And as he changes the altitude of his machine, he
swings like a gyroscope on a pinpoint (except of course he
can go around 360 degrees without tumbling). Where he
is going, in relation to the ground, doesn't matter; it is
only what he does that counts. And so in barrel-rolls or
lazy-eights, you sit co-ordinated on the fixed axis of
nothing, while across the canopy the horizon moves in
sweeping diagonals—coming by your shoulder in a dark
line to dive straight down your nose. Now and then the
sun will cut a bright arc through the pattern, like a
thrown ball. The leading edge of the wings catch the light
and vault slowly above the fulcrum of invisible noise
which is the propeller. A cloud may stain the whole
maneuver white. When you get as good as Norman
Bluhm was, you can do a loop, half-roll out of the bottom
into a split-eight, come up with an Immelman turn and
not only stay perfectly still, but be exactly where you were
in worldly reference to a little crossroad 8,000 feet below.*[54]

Bluhm's energetic painting is often counterbalanced by
the most sobering titles. His enormous rambling yet
ultimately integrated triptych, *Acheron* (fig. 16), recalls
the lower world, the inferno, referring specifically to the
river of sadness in Thresprotia that flowed into the
Cocytus, the river of lamentation. The word *Acheron*
derives from the Greek root for affliction, although the
exuberant painting, coming back upon itself in giant
loops, cannot otherwise be associated with such arcana.
However large a work, Bluhm does not exaggerate the
gesture needed to occupy the canvas and, as a result, his
accurate sense of scale appears unhindered. *Acheron* far
surpasses in controlled drama the earlier triptych, *Aritic*
(cat. no. 1), as Bluhm's development saw no slackening of
his zeal or ambitions. Rushes of energetic painting—
that in their freshness depend on the precedent of Pollock or late Gorky—alternating with oases of calm,

signal that Bluhm is dealing in an art of judicious oppo-
sitions; color schemes range from the highest to deepest
values, hue is varied, and scale, however grand, manages
to attract our attention to the finer aspects of painthandling. Through a long arid period of little critical
support Bluhm continued his work; long after the public
had lost its first infatuation with abstract expressionism, he was seen to be working "in what many assume to
be a dead style."[55]

The giant *Thamyris* (fig. 17) refers to a Thracian
bard—the son of Philammon who was said to be the son
of Apollo—who instituted choral dances at Delphi.
Thamyris was the first man to fall in love with Hyacin-
thus, but when Thamyris challenged the Muses at song
in a contest at Dorium in Messenia he lost, was struck
blind and dumb, and after death was cast among the
presumptuous in Tartarus. (The story seems to be the
kernel from which sprang Thomas Mann's *Death in
Venice*.) The size of the canvas exceeds the widest gesture of the human frame; this surface, almost like a
boxing ring, is capable of containing *any* action, and
Bluhm's titles hint that the dark side of mythology
attracted him.

One of Jackson's most remarkable exhibitions,
although none could have known it at the time, was a
show of Morris Louis's work that ran at the gallery
during November 1957.[56] This was the artist's first one-
man show in New York and proved to be the only
exhibition exclusively of his work during his lifetime.
This group of paintings documents his return to a form
of abstract expressionsim that Louis practiced *after* his
first accomplishment with stain painting; the new technique so unnerved Louis that he retreated to the relative
security of the earlier style. Clement Greenberg, the
eminent critic and Louis's intimate counselor, selected a
number of these paintings to be sent to the gallery where

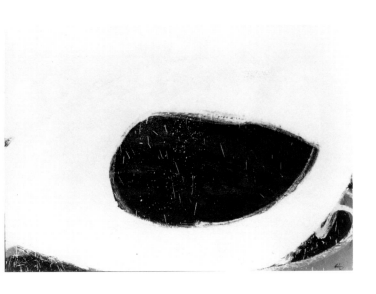

they were unrolled by Martha Jackson and Michel Tapie, both of whom instantly had their curiosity aroused concerning this essentially unknown artist. They drove to Washington, D.C., to visit Louis, and following their meeting the November exhibition was planned. Tapie bought one of the paintings from the show and had it shipped to Paris; another of the works was selected for the April 1958 Osaka Festival; one became part of the collection of the University of Arizona, Tucson; one is in the Neuberger Collection, Purchase, New York (fig. 18); one was purchased by Martha Jackson and is now part of the collection of the Albright-Knox Art Gallery (fig. 19); and one came to the National Museum of American Art from the Vincent Melzac Collection (fig. 20). Shortly after this exhibition Louis repudiated abstract expressionism forever; he returned to stain painting and destroyed the remaining unsold

Figure 17. Norman Bluhm, *Thamyris*, 1972 (cat. no. 5)

Figure 18. Morris Louis, Untitled, 1956, acrylic on canvas, 83 x 93 in. Neuberger Museum, State University of New York, Purchase, New York. Gift of Roy R. Neuberger.

Figure 19. Morris Louis, "No. 1," 1956–57, oil and metallic paint on canvas, 93½ x 80½ in. Albright-Knox Art Gallery, Buffalo, New York, The Martha Jackson Collection.

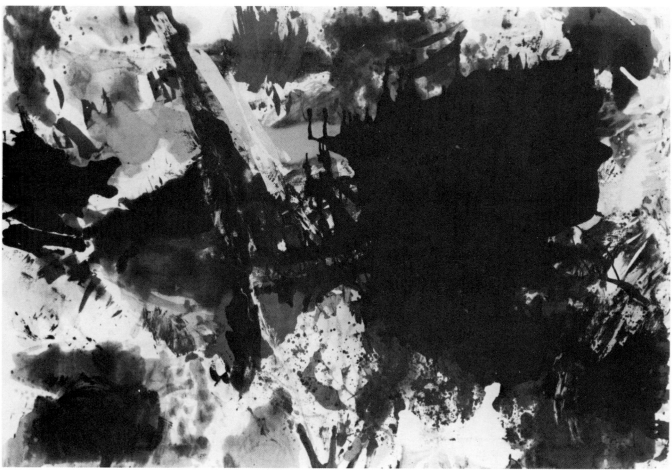

Figure 20. Morris Louis, Untitled, 1956, oil and acrylic on canvas, 75¾ x 106 in. National Museum of American Art, Smithsonian Institution, Washington, D.C., Museum purchase from the Vincent Melzac Collection.

works in the show and all similar paintings in his own holdings.[57] Thus, this slender list of works represents a very special art historical resource. The representation of Louis by Martha Jackson is one of the quieter, if not more moving, chapters of this artist's history.

Generally associated with West Coast painting, Frank Lobdell had a long and fruitful relationship with the gallery. Indeed, his muscular and forbidding painting was given its first thorough exposition not in San Francisco, but in New York. Lobdell recalls:

Martha bought out the 1960 exhibition which allowed me to work when I needed it most, and continued her keen interest in my work: writing often and visiting my studio several times a year. During these years Martha was totally involved in satisfying her curiosity about painting. She traveled all over the world looking for it and at it and this was all I ever heard her talk about. She was a bit obsessed about the subject—the reason I looked forward to her visits and found them so refreshing.[58]

When his works were first seen in the East they met with immediate acceptance. Dore Ashton reviewed Lobdell's first solo exhibition in New York:

He is well known on the West Coast, but for some reason has not penetrated the New York scene. His show should remedy that, for Mr. Lobdell is one of the few San Francisco painters who have been able to take the lessons of Clyfford Still and Mark Rothko, and do something with them.[59]

While Still and Rothko were massively important figures in the development of art in California, much of what was produced in the wake of their teaching, or promoted in their name, was far less decisive than Lobdell's difficult and not so lyrical painting. His works were described as forbidding or somber, but they met, nevertheless, with a sympathetic reception and favorable comparison.

Lobdell's work is less difficult than Still's, but it is less rhetorical too; in fact it is characterized by an earnestness and a mellow, yet intense Romanticism. His colors tend to be dark and brooding, and the eruption of the quasi-forms occurs with a rich glow that one associates with religious work.[60]

Nothing could be more typical of this sort of picture than Lobdell's *December 1958* (fig. 21), a painting that dates from the period directly after his first contact with the gallery. This is a thickly painted work through whose dark brown field eerily glides an irregular band streaked with white. It was precisely of such a piece that Irving Sandler could have written that Lobdell is an artist who "paints somber abstract 'figures' that snake slowly across or up heavily trowelled black or deep brown backgrounds. There is a feeling of sleep in these pictures...."[61] The dark colors seem to describe a world of half-light, brooding, slow, deliberate and ageless. The same crusty paint that gave the textures of geology to

Figure 21. Frank Lobdell, *December 1958*, 1958 (cat. no. 97)

Clyfford Still's landscape shapes, when used by Lobdell, suggested that time had slowed to a geologic pace, and with it light had lost its dominion.

In work such as *Summer 1962* (fig. 22) the same formula of high-value crusty paint and reptilian forms evoked petroglyphs, mute reminders of long-gone personalities. The higher valued colors, the brilliant yellow of the field, does not lighten the tone of the picture; there is nothing festive about such an image. Rather, the same seriousness that was achieved with low-value and low-intensity colors was somehow managed with high-value, high-intensity yellow.

As a young man in New Orleans, Fritz Bultman's family had Morris Graves as a house guest who obligingly showed the youngster something about painting. This auspicious start was reinforced when the young man met Hans Hofmann's wife, Maria, in Munich where he attended preparatory school. He returned to the United States and studied at the New Bauhaus in Chicago in 1937 and with Hofmann in Provincetown, Massachusetts, and New York between 1938 and 1941. Subsequent awards and travel in America and Europe further informed his vision. To the degree that such studies took him afar, Bultman opened himself to the possibility that as an artist

...the further he goes away from his background when he is young, the more severely he severs himself from it in exploring and learning his own nature and talent, the

Figure 22. Frank Lobdell, *Summer 1962*, 1962 (cat. no. 98)

more likely he is to return to it at a certain point and find it richly rewarding subject matter.[62]

Bultman did not consider his own art wholly abstract and relied on the model, which supplied a foundation from which he never strayed very far. For all his cosmopolitan learning Bultman's deep strain of easy southern grace was noticed by many.

Bultman seems to measure the temperature of childhood memories of New Orleans and to transfer the heat (and the humidity) to his canvases....The intensity of these apparently autobiographical works causes them to transcend the particular.[63]

And yet, these observations were made of works that were, for all intents, as non-objective as those of any artist being shown in the gallery, or for that matter in New York. This residual autobiographical strain supplied the generalities of human life from which were distilled the universals of the New York School. Artists as diverse as Gorky and Gottlieb had founded their work on such personal proclivities, while later artists, such as Morris Louis, were able to initiate a work with a technical or compositional incident.

The paintings seem to depend upon Bultman's sureness as a draftsman to supply the basic structure, and particularly in his figurative works—using a surprisingly clear and hard sharp line—he has few contemporary equals. During the 1940s Bultman conceived of his paintings as studies for sculptures, although until he had learned the techniques of building clay forms on wire-mesh armatures in 1950 he did not feel confident enough to work successfully on prolonged sculptural forays.[64] The basic elements of his style were already recognized as a feature of the period to which he belonged: "The upward thrust of Bultman's sculpture, together with its lack of mass, conveys a sensation of lightness (bordering on elation) which is held in check by our knowledge that the material is really heavy."[65] The contemporary viewer can acknowledge that Bultman's sculpture represents a period style, but is, nevertheless, a masterful expression of that vernacular; at the same time, a work like *Azores I* (fig. 23) does have a particular exuberance and balletlike grace. Mounted on its very long support the work appears floral, a floating gesture freed from the ground and dancing in air. That Bultman chose lost wax to develop his sculptural sense—as opposed to construction, for example—was a telling decision that affected the appearance of his work; he is "attracted to bronze which has both liquid and solid states. Bronze can flow at the demand of gravity or solidly resist."[66] Attempted in another material (other abstract expressionist sculpture hardly looks like Bultman's), he could not have achieved this gestural aspect.

His paintings of this period, although not obviously sculptural, embed a strong form within a churning atmospheric field. A painting such as *The Delta* (fig. 24) is a contemporary of the bronze *Azores I*; however, without the additional knowledge supplied by Bultman's statement of a unified conception for his paintings and sculpture, it would be hard to assign these works to the

Figure 24. Fritz Bultman, *The Delta,* 1959 (cat. no. 12)

same artist. The sensibility the two works share—that firm central form, clearly defined and rising from a single central support—reminds us that had Franz Kline produced sculpture it might well have resembled Bultman's. With the exception of some early ceramic pieces by Pollock, Barnett Newman's supremely moving works, and the late sculptures of Adolph Gottlieb, few New York School painters also worked as sculptors. Therefore, these bronzes by Bultman open a door to otherwise unheralded possibilities.

Bultman's statements about drawing, as impassioned as the works themselves, allow us to gauge something of the thought and rigor that he brings to his draftsmanship. Describing a piece like *Miki (Oriental II)* (fig. 25) Bultman gives essential insights into his works.

It might seem a contradiction that during a life spent painting and sculpting the abstract image, I should spend so much time drawing the figure, but I have always drawn from nature. There is the robustness, variety, and richness of the physical world I want to carry over to my abstract painting and sculpture....I am old fashioned enough to believe in experience and believe that each work

Figure 23. Fritz Bultman, *Azores I,* 1959 (cat. no. 11)

23

Figure 25. Fritz Bultman, *Miki (Oriental II)*, 1964 (cat. no. 13)

grounded in the experience of the artist should start at the beginning....Each time that I start to draw from the figure it is beginning all over again....Everything is learning, and if one thinks one knows, then the end has passed.[67]

The refinement of the shapes' firm borders brings Matisse (particularly the early reclining *Blue Nude*) to mind, although Bultman's work possesses a certain stringency wholly atypical of the French (or even of French New Orleans). This rigor, so un-Mediterranean and un-Southern, is easier to associate with Bultman's Germanic schooling. Were it not for the surety of his handling of drawn edges, we would not feel as confident in our appreciation of his collages which, like Matisse's, are not *collage* in the cubist tradition, but *papiers decoupés* (cuttings made into papers that have first been painted—a technique perfected by Matisse). Matisse likened his *papiers decoupés* to sculpting in pure color, carving color into shapes without substance.

Bultman has written forcefully about the sources of his notions concerning collage:

I took the painting of papers with gouache from Matisse's cut-outs, but I began to work anew in collage from a center outward, rather than working on the confines of a sheet of paper. By adding piece to piece I find a means that gives me a collage of random shape through random growth, more like the wax sculptures I made out of the pieces of wax joined one to the other. The relationship to sculpture and to shape is more deliberate because of the emphasis on thingness, and also on contour, that knifes through space and carries the form on beyond its immediate visual limits.[68]

Describing a work such as *The Way Up and The Way Down* (fig. 26), Hilton Kramer remarked that Bultman's collages "are almost prodigal in their brilliance. Composed of bright, gouache-colored papers that have been cut and pasted into images of celebration, these collages

24

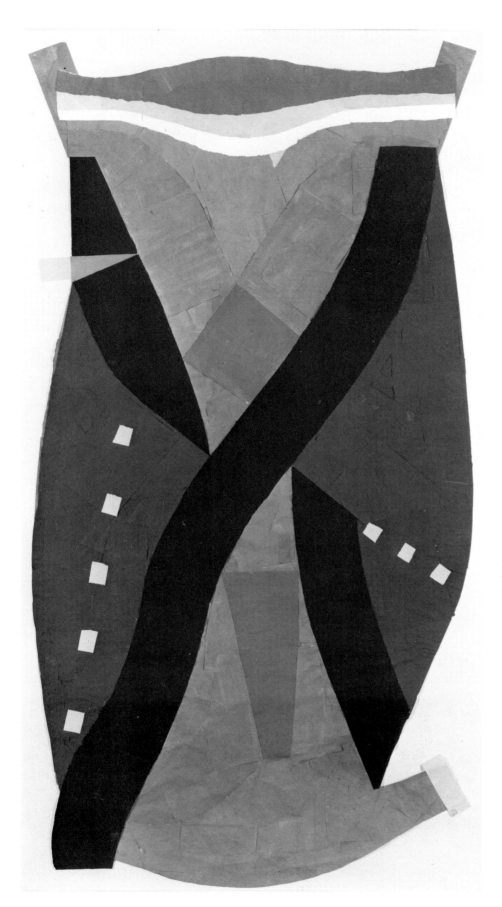

Figure 26. Fritz Bultman,
The Way Up and the Way Down, 1975
(cat. no. 15)

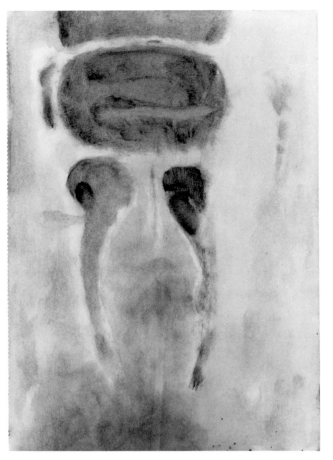

Figure 27. Sam Francis, Untitled, ca. 1948–50 (cat. no. 33)

Figure 28. Sam Francis, Untitled, 1951 (cat. no. 34)

are large in their gestures and overflow with the kind of feelings we miss in sculpture."[69] Indeed, some critics also found this comparison with sculpture apt.

> *Martha Jackson made full use of its large space…divided into moveable walls. There were two sculptures by Fritz Bultman….Relationships with the accompanying group of his collages were obvious. Organic shapes filled in with flat colors form creatures or map-like patterns; one, for instance, connotes* The Way Up and the Way Down. *Small squares are incorporated on the busy surface seemingly to act as windows of entry.*[70]

Others, more excited still, remarked on the collages' "monumental size (some are eight feet high), sensuous shapes and exuberant red, blue and gold acrylic colors. These works vie with the heroicism of New York School painting and sculpture."[71]

Of the West Coast artists that Martha Jackson brought to New York, certainly the most celebrated and ultimately the most successful was a painter whose reputation was well established in Europe before Americans paid him much heed. Sam Francis was born in San Mateo, California, and studied medicine and psychology at the University of California at Berkeley; in 1943 as a pilot for the Army Air Corps he suffered a serious spinal injury. Confined in a hospital for months, immobile except for his head and arms, he abandoned any thought of becoming a doctor and took up painting. In a wheelchair he visited the California Palace of the Legion of Honor and saw El Greco's *St. Peter*, of which he recalled, "It knocked me out….I probably would have died if it had not been for painting….The picture by El Greco changed my life."[72] On his release from the hospital he studied painting with David Park, painted his first abstract work in 1947, received his B.A. and M.A. in art from Berkeley, and moved to Paris in 1950 where he studied briefly at the Academie Fernand Léger and had a painting in the VI Salon de Mai in Paris. Soon after arriving he established friendships with Al Held, Norman Bluhm, Joan Mitchell, and John Hultberg—future Martha Jackson artists.

Some of Francis's earliest abstract works reflect the most alluring influences on a young artist at the end of the 1940s and also hint at his future artistic direction. A small untitled watercolor from about 1948 (fig. 27) echoes the warm colors and floating fields of Rothko's paintings at that time. Although Francis's piece is a watercolor and Rothko worked in oils, there is, nevertheless, a similar treatment of the thin muted colors. For a youthful artist separated from the heady exchanges of New York, such a salute was a bold expression of admiration. Yet these bouyant shapes also possess certain anatomical references, more characteristic of Gorky than the land-, sea-, and skyscapes of Rothko, and such an elision of styles suggests the terrific appetite with which Francis consumed the best of contemporary art. The stain-painting technique that appears in this work, perhaps an experiment, foreshadows the major technical theme of his career.

For example, in another untitled work, which is inscribed "April 1951" on the back (fig. 28), the liquid property of the ink brushed on wet paper presages Francis's later work—as well as the stain paintings of Morris Louis, Helen Frankenthaler, and a host of others. At the same time the wet field contributed suggestions of aerial perspective as well as recalling a grand geological scale. In this work, too, the hazy background suggests an atmospheric envelope supporting, enrobing and hence lending the form a gigantic aspect (and incidentally producing a shape that was favored by Morris Louis in his early work (figs. 18, 19, 20) and his later *Veils*, a shape that was created by running liquid paint and one that recalled phenomena of enormous size). The edge of Francis's little ink on paper anchors the work with a stripe that would later become the hallmark of such artists as Barnett Newman, who employed the stripe to suggest galactic distance, and Jules Olitski, whose stripes reaffirmed the surface of his paintings in spite of their atmospheric depth. In short, in the early years of his career Francis was working at a furious pace, assaying much of what would become the central agenda of recent painting. The tremendous speed with which Francis acquired the tools of his new profession was noted by Hilton Kramer:

He acted upon the cues gleaned in the work of Rothko and Still with remarkable alacrity and speed. By 1950, before he was thirty, Mr. Francis had more or less mastered the new style of large-scale abstract painting based on heavy saturations of color.[73]

Another small untitled ink and watercolor from 1950 (fig. 29) is a work of astonishing prescience that prefigures much that was to become the hallmark of his major works. In this piece appear those broken touches of color that later—greatly magnified in size by their application to canvas by a sponge—would announce Francis's signature painting style. In addition, this early watercolor contains the strong suggestion of a figure, or the atavistic shapes that indicates such a presence; the reductionist aesthetic for such a compositional devise allies Francis at this stage of his development to Gorky and de Kooning more strongly than to any other American or European counterparts. Founding his art upon that of Rothko, Still, and Gorky, he was welcomed in France where his work was sought and widely exhibited.

Figure 29. Sam Francis, Untitled, 1950–53 (cat. no. 35)

Included in the 1955 Carnegie International, he did not have an American one-man show until 1956—at the Martha Jackson Gallery. (That same year he had a solo exhibition at David Anderson's Paris Galerie Rive Droite and was included in the Museum of Modern Art's *Twelve Americans*.) Since that time his reputation has continued to grow, and he now looms as a major figure of postwar American art, albeit far more famous in Europe where he is regarded as one of the foremost American modern artists.

Americans, never quite able to place this painter, rejected the notion of a Pacific School as a European, mainly French, stylistic confection made to soothe the Gallic sense of history. Francis's work, despite museum exhibitions and support from dealer's has not really been assimilated into a native vision of recent American art. Some basic texts have argued tortuously for his alignment with the New York School, which requires exegetical adriotness of a high order.[74] His art's evolution resembled developments that were occurring independently on the other side of the Atlantic. Francis's approach to a form of abstract expressionism blossomed from an intense rapid education in California, but was cultivated in very different circumstances from what many of his contemporaries knew.[75] In *Black Rectangle*

27

Figure 30. Sam Francis, *Black Rectangle*, 1953 (cat. no. 36)

(fig. 30), a modest work executed in 1953, Francis's major format—a variegated shield of color—had already coalesced from the naturalistic elements on which it depended. Not quite opaque to the point of being impenetrable, but silhouetted with a slight halation that, even when dry-brushed, recalled his experiments with stain painting, the central rectangle satisfied both the requirements for an object-field relationship as well as an all-over composition. This fusion of technique and design has served him well, with variations in motif, to the present day; sometimes the field opened the center, sometimes it was closed, or sometimes sections of a field were presented racing through the picture as stripes.

Francis's untitled work of 1965 (fig. 31) presents the antitheses to many of the propositions of his earlier pieces. Where they had dark, dense centers, this painting is vacant, and brightly so. Where they had been small and hoarded their imagery, this painting extends the rectangular deployment of shape to a size beyond that of a human gesture. If his colors had been complex, almost canceling one another, now they stood out as single, hardly variegated, hues covering great swaths of space.

Although they came from utterly different backgrounds, one of the strongest bonds Martha Jackson ever established was the friendship with Louise Nevelson. Nevelson had been born in Kiev at the turn of the

century and came to Maine with her family in 1905. Between 1929 and 1930 she studied at the Art Students League with Kenneth Hayes Miller, and in 1931 she became a pupil of Hans Hofmann. In the early 1930s Nevelson began exhibiting her work and, toward the end of the following decade, made all-important archeological trips to Central and South America. Only in the 1950s did she begin to have solo exhibitions, and, as Nevelson recalls, Martha Jackson was one of her strongest supporters.

> When Martha opened her gallery it was a very fertile time in New York City. She was one of the first who felt moved to open a gallery and she had a great deal of feeling for artist's creativity. Our relationship was one of mutual respect and feeling. We often traveled together and valued each other's company. We traveled to Haiti, Mexico and California. Martha let me do exactly what I wanted to do. She was alert and open-minded—a great individualist.[76]

A piece like *World Garden Cabinet* (fig. 32) typifies much of the sculptor's work in the mid- to late 1950s. This tall rectangular box, painted entirely black, features an ornamented lid that consists of plywood strips with holes set next to a heavy dowel with small sticks fastened to the front. This ensemble opens from the right to reveal many vertical sticks, inside the box, appended to the inside of the door, also painted black. Near the top, the box has a carved furniture support, an irregular and T-shaped form, as well as a wheel attached to the flat top from which appear nails with exposed points. It was precisely such work that Dore Ashton described as Nevelson's "characteristically vertical boxes with their half-obscured contents and doors slightly ajar [that] played on essential emotions grouped around secrecy, hidden riches and sorrows."[77] Although they recalled treasure, such works were composed of the detritus of city living, as the broken and scuffed lower corner or *World Garden Cabinet* attests. Each piece caught her eye, singled out by the sculptor's underlying sense of taste; this represents the initial, unifying selection of elements.

Later, the particular compositional requirements of a work would further unify these disparate elements as they were compounded into a sculpture whose many separate forms were covered with a single color. Monochromy erased the various sources, the weathering, and accidental scruffs, and the biographical details of each of the units were submerged in a common identity. Whatever the volumetric interest of the final piece, this approach is genuinely sculptural in its deemphasis of color. If such accretive work descended ultimately from cubism, through Gonzalez's assembled sculpture and accumulative/constructivist welders like David Smith, coming finally to Nevelson by way of dada and Kurt Schwitters, little of this heritage was revealed in her work. The weathering that the wood had undergone,

Figure 31. Sam Francis, Untitled, 1965 (cat. no. 38)

the variety of finishes, and the diverse shapes bespoke a universe akin to, but somehow not identical with, our own; in such work we witnessed an oddly distorted mirror image of that antlike industry by which our busy species recognizes itself. The abandoned form mutely attests to anonymous efforts of what Martin Friedman called Nevelson's "phantom architecture."

> *...if such enigmatic shapes inevitably suggest the antique and the dream world, it is the living city's forms that give meaning to her art....If Nevelson's sculpture evokes the city's forms, it does not suggest its kinetic quality.*[78]

The many origins of the works' materials are individually complex, and when shown in groups the sculptures' complexity increased. This was noted by the critics who observed, "If ever there was a metaphoric sculptor it is Louise Nevelson. Her dusky wood constructions, exhibited in a dramatic ensemble at the Martha Jackson Gallery, are eloquent symbols...."[79]

Figure 32. Louise Nevelson, *World Garden Cabinet*, 1959 (cat. no. 104)

Figure 33. Louise Nevelson, *Gate V (Garden Gate Series)*, 1959–60 (cat. no. 105)

Exhibitions of Nevelson's works multiplied the total number of constituent elements; she began to gather mute choirs as she had once scavenged for units of single works, each already composed of her basic found forms. The boxes that had appeared to be "transcendentally obsessive nostalgia for shipment" started to appear "like the contents of a gigantic warehouse where the ghost of Emily Dickinson is expected at any moment."[80] A single substance, bronze—especially well-suited to accretive methods of working toward a final unified product, regardless of original materials—by its distinctive rich color and its single porous surface texture further united the various elements more forcefully than was possible by any wash of paint. The *Gate V (Garden Gate Series)* (fig. 33) exemplifies this accumulation of materials, further elided within the identity of a new material. After casting this sculpture in an edition of three, Nevelson incorporated the piece in her only bronze wall. Perhaps not as sculpturally successful as the smaller units of which it is composed, this larger ensemble from 1961 completes the process of gathering and transforming her mean materials. (See fig. 34.)

While Martha Jackson's taste was inclined toward the abstract expressionists, occasionally a younger artist of apparently different temperament caught her eye, although often such seeming lapses later turned out to have a subterranean continuity, invisible to the casual spectator. Such was her interest in the precocious Jim Dine, who recalls:

> When I was young, 20 years ago, Mrs. Jackson came to me and offered $4000 for me to stop teaching. (I was making $4000 a year teaching elementary school.) She wanted paintings and drawings, $100 for paintings, $25 for drawings. Now that seems like she really got some bargain but in fact I was the winner as I was able to stop teaching and to paint! I remember her fondly as a very eccentric woman who loved art. The Valiant Red Car *was a celebration of her Red Valiant. It was a way for me to depict our relationship without giving up my own iconography. It coincided with a car crash I had.*[81]

The painting (fig. 35) has figured prominently in histories of the period. In retrospect one can see that, like Goldberg's *Sardines*, the *Valiant Red Car* had been eclipsed in size by more recent painting (fig. 36). While it may have felt like a monumental undertaking to Dine, those large areas and the glowering red center of the picture were soon dwarfed by the subsequent evolution of painting. What compelled the relatively large size of this work was the insistent personal meaning that it held for the artist, whose usual attention to a motif or theme has been remarkably short as he moved from one subject to another. Only the autobiographical statement of this piece could have enlarged his ambition to this degree. In fact, the traumatic incident that prompted the oil painting inspired a number of works, such as his print *The Crash #2* (fig. 37) that repeats the turbulent

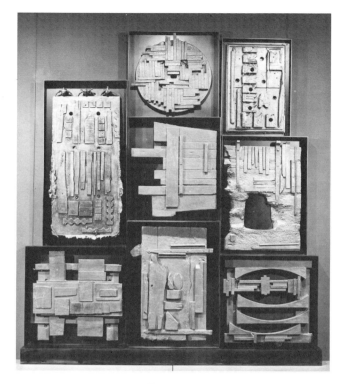

Figure 34. Louise Nevelson, *Illumination-Dark*, 1961, wall of eight bronze reliefs, 125 x 108½ x 5 in. Dedicated and given to the Whitney Museum of American Art, New York, New York, by the artist.

cruciform imagery of the painting. The scrawled black tangle from which emerges the word *crash*—screeching half of an apocalyptic resurrection in concert with the cross, half a comic book sound effect—carries the oddest burden of double meaning that seems oddly suitable to, and makes inventive use of, the print medium. Together these works constituted the *Crash* series.

Such works preceded the period during which Dine, conveniently if incorrectly, was dubbed a pop artist. The *Valiant Red Car* marks that moment when Dine's fundamental character was most accessible to the spectator. An overlay of pop's hipness, its stance of diminished caring and aloof independence, would subsequently obscure the artist's motives and seriousness until, in recent years, his focused intensity has again emerged.[82] His sensibilities were rarely those of true pop art with its basically humorous and irresponsible camp aesthetic. Even Dine's citations of diverse symbol systems in contiguous play were never meant as a spoof on art itself, unlike pop.

> Where language intrudes in his early work, it is not for any whimsical purposes, nor is it like the celebratory puns of Picasso in his Cubist works. [In] the Valiant Red Car... we have a vast theatrical parade of crosses and a mortuary field interrupted by a glowing image like an automobile tire. Above the field of crosses, a negative grid system if ever there were one, is the big funereal epigram "The Val-

Figure 35. Jim Dine, *The Valiant Red Car*, 1960 (cat. no. 26)

iant Red Car". One thinks of Frank O'Hara's "For James Dean" with its colloquial rage: "Welcome me, if you will/ as the ambassador of a hatred/ who knows its cause."[83]

Dine's creativity was the sort that lept with casual pleasure from one image to the next, occasionally arrested on some motif that would focus his attentions for a protracted period before he moved on to another wholly unpredictable theme or image.

Most notable, even notorious, of Martha Jackson's exhibitions was her *New Forms—New Media* (actually two shows that ran in June and September of 1960). These exhibitions set the tone for the decade, perhaps inadvertently, even though Martha Jackson never thought of the art displayed in this major exhibition as equal to the two generations of her much-beloved New York School.

Rosalind Constable begins the story.

In 1960 I was putting together a report on the new "junk" artists, at that time exhibiting at the little downtown Reuben Gallery. In the course of a discussion with Martha she decided to bring the Junk artists uptown. It was a bold step....

Most of the junk art she showed has long since dis- integrated or been destroyed by the artist. But the

Figure 36. Martha Jackson and Rosalind Constable at *Store Days*, Oldenburg/Dine Gallery, lower East Side, during *Car Crash* perform- ance, November 1, 1960. Background: Jim Dine, *The Valiant Red Car* (cat. no. 26).

Figure 37. Jim Dine, *The Crash #2*, 1960, lithograph on paper, 21¼ x 18³/₁₆ in. (image). National Museum of American Art, Smithsonian Institution, Washington, D.C., Museum purchase.

exhibitions included many future Pop artists (Oldenburg, Dine, Indiana), Happening impressarios (Kaprow, Whitman, Brecht) and even future Minimalists (Bladen, Flavin). In fact the seeds of almost every art movement of the sixties were contained in those two exhibitions.[84]

This exhibition opened new territory that Jackson chose to assimilate into her wide embrace of modern art, rather than capitalize on for instant notoriety. John Goodyear recollected that

Martha was a grand but stylishly eccentric gallery director. She did what she wanted to do. People say she could have cornered the market in Pop Art, but she probably just didn't want it.[85]

Her reaction to what became a bonanza of press coverage was not typical of dealers. Contemporary viewers seemed to recognize the special position of her gallery with regard to the art it was then showing out of duty to taste and intellectual honesty. Even the press thought this event newsworthy, if a bit unsettling for the time.

The variety of the junk, or new media, pressed into the service of the new art, made the plush Martha Jackson Gallery look like a swap shop....One is obliged to admire the unworldliness of an artist who goes to great pains to produce a work of art that no collector could buy even if

he wanted to, since it would probably disintegrate on the way home....If proof were needed that Paris now looks to New York for a lead, it could be found in the fact that junk culture has just reached Paris, where it is called "Culture du Debris."[86]

Other dealers might have tapped this vein of novelty for every possible sale, even though most of the criticism was not favorable. In particular, the *New York Times*'s John Canaday excoriated the new work, placing the frivolity of the art in contrasting opposition to the grim responsibility of world leadership in politics and industry.

You knew that not far away from you men from all over the world were trying to find means to preserve their countries, their continents and their world, possibly even our planet. Then you reached the gallery, and there you found a bunch of artists playing at sticking string on paper and spraying it white, at covering the surface of a mirror with tacks, glued on head down, at cutting out crudely drawn paper dolls and hanging them from chicken wire, at ripping old nylon stockings and stretching them across odds and ends of wire or stuffing them with trash and tying the ends with string like nasty sausages. The air of the gallery seemed to be filled with little shrieks of perverse delight, and you were ashamed to be there and a part of it.[87]

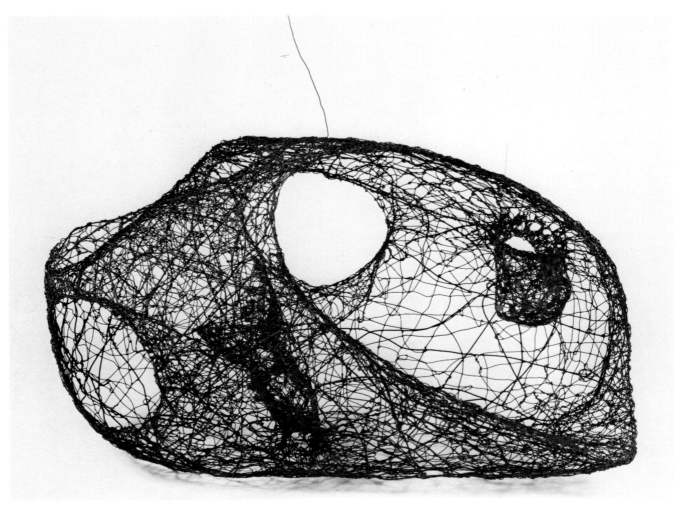

Figure 38. Claire Falkenstein, *Envelope*, 1958 (cat. no. 30)

In particular, Canaday took the artists and the gallery to task for what he thought was their aping of a gone dada tradition that was based on the liberating influence of Freud, the protest of an earlier generation's furious exasperation with World War I, and the exhaustion of every rational means of expression "against a world that seemed to have gone mad or senile." In the spirit of an honest, if an enraged report, he did offer a sympathetic insight into this situation expressed by the exhibition. To capture the spirit in which this exhibition was received, it is worth noting that Canaday saw these artists as striving to overcome the glut of images that spewed forth from the many forms of photographic reproduction and that in these circumstances

the artist is left to scavenge for whatever means he can find to re-establish himself as a creator, to disassociate his product from the familiar images of the camera and the machine. His hope is to discover an anti-photographic and mechanically unreproduceable technique of expression....[88]

It was paradoxically at the moment of her greatest celebrity that Jackson's intuition, born of a particular

generation's taste, reached its crest. If the *New York Times* of the early 1960s supplied a strident forum for dour critics of this new art, a dozen years later a gentler reviewer noted the changing character of that moment and observed from the perch of the 1970s that Martha Jackson "...recoiled from most Pop art...and Post-Painterly Abstraction. This raucous new work must have struck her at the time as positively hostile to everything she liked best in art. In any case, she rejected it, and it was at this point that her gallery...lost its art world cachet."[89] As time passed, her accomplishment grew in stature and critics noted a kind of aesthetic self-immolation that this pivotal show represented for the gallery, even as it advanced art history.

I admire the openness, or at least the preparedness, with which such a committed and understanding enthusiast of Abstract Expressionism as Martha Jackson took to Pop Art. She took most readily to painterly Pop—to Olden-burg, and to the mock-Expressionism in Dine, and natu-rally to the stradling style of Rivers. But that's fine as far as it goes: the reason why something is wrong is more important than the reason why something is right. The

34

only trouble is that as the 60s passed from dawn to noon, errors of inclusion begin to multiply [in her collecting]. As we move through the last decade we bump into a number of relatively undistinguished works. It is just conceivable that these may one day prove just as acute intuitions as Martha Jackson's earlier insights....[90]

An artist whose work was to partake of all the joyful irreverence that the coming decade offered and who was to contribute to its possibilities with her neon-tube sculpture, was the Greek-born (Vardea) Chryssa. In the second edition of *New Forms—New Media* she exhibited a piece called *White Relief* (cat. no. 22), a work in which only the most discerning observer would have noticed in the blinking rhythm of white knobs this artist's potential for the luminous and sometimes monumental works that followed from this preliminary experimental form. After this piece was executed and exhibited at the Martha Jackson Gallery, Chyrssa's work took on that character by which it is best known; this early piece is therefore a valuable document of her sense of form operating without electricity. By the next year, after the *New Forms—New Media* show, her talent was established, and she enjoyed a solo exhibition at the Guggenheim Museum.

Another of the West Coast artists whom Martha Jackson met in Europe and subsequently showed in New York was Claire Falkenstein. Falkenstein's major contribution to sculpture occurred in 1954, when, while working in Rome, she discovered a means of fusing metal and glass. The volume of a substantial, if transparent, form (glass) could be opposed by the inert substance of ductile metal, drawn thin as wires or combined in rods to swoop, curling through space. Substance was made transparent, solids made insubstantial. This technique represented a natural means to advance constructivist sculpture, and it was not long before she started to exploit this potential. A long-time confidante of Martha Jackson's, Michel Tapie, remarked that

... the space enclosed plays as important a role as that outside. In her hands the webs become almost a raw material, created to fit her needs, that she either hollows out, or hammers, or welds along lines of stress and at essential points with great architectural lyricism and baroque profusion of inventiveness.[91]

Envelope (fig. 38) seems an airy web and dates from the period of her first experiments with fused glass and metal. The formal logic implicit in its nebulous shape barely weds such a work to the tradition established by Naum Gabo or Antoine Pevsner, who are certainly the work's spiritual ancestors; yet, this piece diverged from the constructivist mainstream. Without recourse to a rigorous geometry of namable shapes, *Envelope* engages the major themes of constructivist sculpture. Pockets in the surface describe a complex plane which, together with the openings into the center of the form, provide an

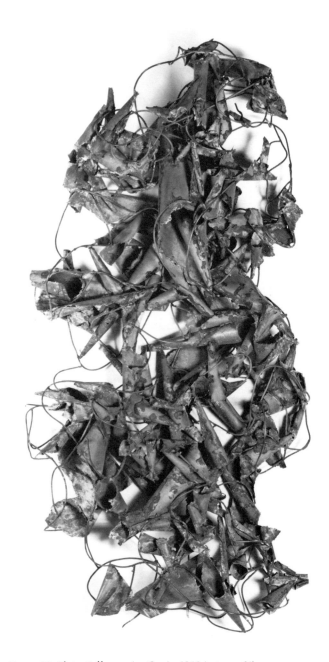

Figure 39. Claire Falkenstein, *Conic*, 1959 (cat. no. 31)

essay in topology. Exterior surfaces dip into the heart of the piece to become interiors that rise again to the surface. Additionally, the piece can be suspended by a wire from its top so that it can be viewed from every side and not just the 360 degrees available from circumambulation. To the degree that the work consciously and systematically examines every possible permutation of surface, it does fully explore the spatial *Envelope* and earn its name. So complex are these situations that spatial relationships in the piece resemble those found in living organisms; like living things *Envelope* is not wedded to a base.

Figure 40. Claire Falkenstein, *Corona*, 1971 (cat. no. 32)

By the next year a new focus came into her work. Real severity never characterizes any of Falkenstein's joyful and energetic sculpture, which always seems expressive before it shows its theoretical underpinning. *Conic* (fig. 39) assays the possibilities of an animated high-relief sculpture executed in brazed copper. Around the central mass of accumulated cones, wire performs as draftsmanship, analogous to abstract expressionist painting. The forms tumbling across its surface hardly seem in disarray, instead *Conic* complements the architecture against which and from which it arises. To the degree that it makes us conscious of the plane of the wall, this portable sculpture feels more a mural than many a painting of a much larger size.[92]

By the early 1970s Falkenstein extended her formal vocabulary with the free execution typified by *Corona* (fig. 40), a jewel that freely mixes colored passages of glass with an equal volume of open space. The compact spaces that flow throughout the whole sculpture here become the transparent volume that glinting shards of colored glass had once been. Unified, the three elements of metals, glass, and space take on equal roles that perform harmoniously. In this small work, space feels concentrated, as if this were the reduction of a mammoth conception; yet, because of the luxuriant qualities that she elicits from her materials, a sense of smallness and preciousness emerges as the piece's primary sensation.

One of the most remarkable exhibitions mounted by the gallery came about as the result of a theatrical production for which two young artists collaborated. A youthful playwright, then without much reputation, worked with an uncelebrated painter. Kenneth Koch's wry playlet, *George Washington Crossing the Delaware*, was performed Off Broadway at the Maidman Theatre in March 1962. As stage sets for this production Alex Katz manufactured about twenty cutout figures and props. (See fig. 41.) A New Yorker by birth, Katz had been

trained classically, had drawn from plaster casts for years and had worked as a commercial artist—at first doing paste-ups. Katz entered the Cooper Union Art School in 1946 and encountered his first serious training in art, although he was already employed as a commercial artist; his teachers included Peter Busa, Robert Gwathmey, and Morris Kantor. A scholarship allowed him to paint at the Skowhegan School in Maine for a summer, and this experience consolidated his desire to become a fine artist. Continuing to work commercially, he began showing in New York galleries in the early 1950s. In the last years of that decade he produced his first cutouts by slicing the figures he was painting away from the surrounding canvas and mounting them on board; he subsequently began to paint directly on cutout wood shapes. Suggesting the Roman portrait busts he had seen in the Metropolitan Museum, these cutouts recalled effigies.

The cutouts he produced for the Kenneth Koch play were not meant as static elements coldly inserted onto the stage just to support the actors' gesturing. In a statement about the role of these pieces Katz announced:

I do not think that sets or costumes should decorate a play or dance.... Rather they should interpret the spirit and present it as strongly as the play, acting and staging.[93]

Thereafter Katz's flat wooden surfaces, shaped to fit his subject matter, became one of his principal formal means, and this combination of painting and flat sculpture continues as a prominent feature in his work. The sets, as much as the play, created a sensation. Alex Katz recalls that Martha Jackson

located the sets and bought them. The largest sale in my career, $1500, and had an exhibition. I sure appreciated Martha's support—after all, she actually bought my madness and helped make it sane for other people.[94]

Press coverage followed and the sets created a sensation; their presentation in the gallery was hardly less exciting than the works themselves had been as supporting players in a theatrical arrangement. For the exhibition, the complete text of the play was mounted in a photostatically enlarged typescript all around the gallery walls where visitors could match scenes with the figures and savor Koch's benign satire.

The cutouts were not the first such sculptures that Katz produced, but they certainly were the most well received and garnered significant recognition for the young artist, which was largely due to the fine support the gallery rendered in mounting so conspicuous a presentation. A contemporary reviewer pointed out that

These cut-outs are related to the painted flat sculpture shown at the Tanager [Gallery] in February. But they are historically accurate figures and objects, appropriately stylized to suit Koch's parody of a mythic episode. And like Koch's play, they are somewhat in between a linger-

Figure 41. Alex Katz astride *The White Horse* (cat. no. 87).

ing reverence (the cut-outs have a clean dignity)—for it is America after all, and the old history books are still on our top shelves—and a gentle retrospective fun-making.[95]

The pieces (figs. 42, 44-50) played a role in transforming the high seriousness of the New York School's abstraction. Irving Sandler and Bill Berkson in their monograph on Katz called him "a painter who seems to summarize many concerns and assumptions of 'post-abstract' painting."[96] The slow evolution of abstraction seemed poised for a devolution that would unravel its carefully wrought language of surrogate symbols. Rather than treat the problems of the painters who had inherited the awesome patrimony of abstract expressionism, Katz "deals with the problems of form (in terms of the figure-ground relationship) by virtually ignoring them."[97] This diversion of modernist art was not well received in all circles, and the resistance with which the work was met signaled a new moment. The work drew its most

obvious sources not from any immediate predecessor, but from Emanuel Leutze's *Washington Crossing the Delaware* (fig. 43), a painting that approaches the status of a national icon. Countless spectators would recognize the motif of Washington's daring crew in their small boat without being able to name the source or author of that image. Contemporaries who understood Katz's many sly and honorific references, as well as the place the cutouts were making for themselves in history—standing between a monumental artistic generation and another heroic generation (the subject of the play and the cutouts), and the grandiloquent source in Leutze—had their hands full deciding just how serious the young artist was. Whether the work was homage or mockery, a salute or a final gesture of disdain was not easily resolved. Both art and history were discussed in a low vernacular. At the time Irving Sandler quipped that "his show might have been titled 'George Washington Crossing the Delacroix'."[98]

Figure 42. Alex Katz, cutouts (see cat. nos. 84–94) produced for
Kenneth Koch's one-act play, *George Washington Crossing the Delaware*, performed in 1962

Figure 44. Alex Katz, *Japan China Teapot*, (cat. no. 84), with *Two tea cups*, (cat. no. 94)

Figure 45. Alex Katz,
Lantern (cat. no. 85)

Figure 46. Alex Katz,
Table and Cake (cat. no. 86)

Figure 47. Alex Katz,
American Revolutionary Soldier
(cat. no. 88)

Figure 48. Alex Katz,
American Revolutionary Soldier
(cat. no. 93)

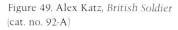

Figure 49. Alex Katz, *British Soldier*
(cat. no. 92-A)

Figure 50. Alex Katz, *British So.*
(cat. no. 92-B)

Figure 43. Emanuel Leutze (1816–68), *Washington Crossing the Delaware*, 1851, oil on canvas, 149 x 255 in. The Metropolitan Museum of Art, New York, New York. Gift of John Stewart Kennedy.

Figure 51. Grace Hartigan, *Frank O'Hara*, 1966, oil on linen, 80⅛ x 80 in. (203.4 x 203.2 cm.). National Museum of American Art, Smithsonian Institution, Washington, D.C. Gift of the artist.

In the wake of the massively important figures who preceded them, younger artists encountered some difficulty in finding an audience. Irving Sandler dates the beginning of their acceptance in 1956 when

...the museum [the Museum of Modern Art] "officially" accepted four second-generation painters—[Ernest] Briggs, [Sam] Francis, [Grace] Hartigan, and [Larry] Rivers—by including them in a "Twelve Americans" show. This event probably more than any other signaled—as it contributed to—the arrival of the younger New York School artists.[99]

Grace Hartigan was one of the few in her generation whose work was sanctioned by earlier exhibitions (fig. 51). As early as 1950 Hartigan had been selected by Meyer Schapiro and Clement Greenberg to participate in the benchmark exhibition, *New Talent*, at the Samuel Kootz Gallery; in 1952 she collaborated with Frank O'Hara on a series of poem-paintings. The poet's suite of twelve poems called *Oranges* was published by the Tibor de Nagy Gallery in 1953 on the occasion of Hartigan's exhibition of her *Oranges* paintings. That same

Figure 52. Grace Hartigan, *Modern Cycle*, 1967 (cat. no. 44)

year the Museum of Modern Art purchased one of her works for its permanent collection. Grace Hartigan began exhibiting at the Martha Jackson Gallery in 1962, although her informal association with the gallery—as part of the world in which artists, critics, dealers, art historians, collectors, and curators swim in schools—predated her business relationship. Hartigan recalled:

I always went to her openings, they were exciting—and, important to artists, she served free liquor. We did become friends, she stayed with my late husband and me in Maine and Baltimore, and I stayed with her in New York.

It is hard to describe her special complexity, she was so acute—sharp—and often seemed so vague. I remember being with Larry Rivers, where Larry was convinced she was completely oblivious to what we were saying, but I kept on with it knowing full well an hour or so later she could repeat verbatim what had gone on....Her devotion to "her" artists was remarkable. She went through some good times with me, and when my work was rejected with most other "abstract expressionists," some bad times. But she never stopped supporting me both economically and emotionally.[100]

When Hartigan moved to Baltimore in the mid-1960s she began to find her subject matter in the streets and the rugged vivacious activity of the city. It was from this period that Hartigan's painting *Modern Cycle* (fig. 52) arrives, brimming with references to the world in which she moved. A teacher, she sympathized with the youthful enthusiasms of her charges. The "second generation" had ceased to be mere junior partners. *Modern Cycle* suggests a detached and poetically melancholic view of the world.

When Martha died I was under financial obligation to the gallery and David Anderson selected works of mine to meet my debt. In 1967 I had become artist-in-residence at the Maryland Institute College of Art's Hoffberger School of Graduate Painting. My male students at the time were obsessed with motorcycles—one even kept his in his studio—out of sheer self-preservation I bought a poster of Brando on a bike and Peter Fonda, some cycle magazines, pinned them on my painting wall and Modern Cycle was the result. It is one of my favorite paintings.[101]

Figure 53. Lester Johnson, *Two Heads: Red*, 1961 (cat. no. 76)

Lester Johnson was hardly a typical abstract expressionist. A prominent artist in New York, Johnson was very much a part of the 8th Street artists' club as well as the 10th Street artists' co-op movement. He was among the first to seek out loft spaces on the Lower East Side after he arrived in New York in 1947. Johnson first met Martha Jackson

...at the opening of her first gallery in New York....She was showing de Kooning Women *paintings which she had just purchased. At that time I painted in my apartment on 95th Street and 3rd Avenue....Martha came, immediately liked my work which she had already seen at the Korman Gallery and offered to buy some early Chicago gouaches. However, she did not offer me a show which is what I wanted and didn't want to sell the Chicago gouaches so nothing came of the visit. About five years later...I received a letter from her asking to talk to me. Soon after she...offered me a contract.*

A nice part of being in her gallery was feeling that she was committed to my work and supported it wholeheart-

edly at a time when people were not ready for figurative expressionism.[102]

Johnson was an abstract painter until 1954 when he started to capture the essence of the city. He painted the quick tempo of those who lived out impersonal careers amid skyscrapers and never looked up, the slouched gait of the inured urbanite, and aggressively beautiful women (those the tabloids would call "statuesque"). These characteristics abound in both the subject matter and the formal properties of his work. The smoldering dark color of *Two Heads: Red* (fig. 53) presses its low-intensity colors directly against the picture plane. Nothing could be more different from establishing depth with aerial perspective's gray/white tonality than this barely visible color scheme that ominously impresses two figures upon the foremost areas of the picture.

The same menacing and looming figures of his early work continued to appear in pictures like *Broadway*

Figure 54. Lester Johnson, *Broadway Street Scene*, 1962 (cat. no. 77)

Street Scene (fig. 54), with its scrawled message. An opaque screen of three men, shoulder to shoulder, blocks the foreground of the picture; nothing about the hats, indistinct faces, thick necks, and wide-shouldered bodies individuates these figures. They serve as the most forceful and impenetrable contrast to the immaterial script—"blue"— that's scrawled across the central surface. In an unusual work, *Beethoven with Stove* (fig. 55), Johnson, who rarely positioned a figure completely contained by the enframing edge (an unexpected inheritance of Impressionism), situated the two subjects well within the boundary of the canvas. In the foreground heavily outlined in black, a potbellied stove stands to the left of a bust of Beethoven; neither shape is modeled to record light and shadow. The basic themes of his career were recounted in the reviews of his first solo show at the Martha Jackson Gallery.

What apples were to Cézanne the figure is to Johnson. He uses it to explore a host of complex relationships, some having to do with the fact of human presence....Whatever Johnson discovers about his life is described in a stark and hermetic idiom. He usually paints thick, viscous atmosphere in which the profiles of his figures stand with hieratical stillness....In his most recent canvases, Johnson experiments with the written word which he scrawls over his compositions with the same free stroke that is the basis for his style. [103]

His combination of scrawled words and robust figuration was a generation ahead of his time and still is today. At the time, it was commonplace for artists (de Kooning for example) to efface their occasional use of letters and words in the process of arriving at an abstract whole. Thus, Frank O'Hara's description of Michael Goldberg at work recalls that method by which painters gradually obliterated words and images until only a hint of the work's original linear armature peeks through. In contrast to this method of using language as an associational tool—to be rubbed out or covered by subsequent

43

Figure 55. Lester Johnson, *Beethoven with Stove*, 1964 (cat. no. 79)

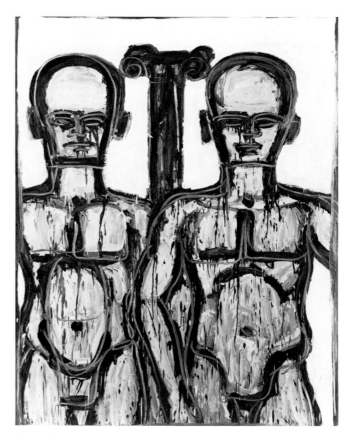

Figure 56. Lester Johnson, *Two Self Portraits*, 1965 (cat. no. 80)

painting—Johnson often applied his writing atop an otherwise finished work in which a compositional area had been reserved for the words, or, alternatively, the letters mingled within the painting's interior space, jostling for parity with the figures. Characteristically, the word *blue* that sometimes appears in his works is not written in that color but invokes it by denotion. Johnson's *Two Self Portraits* (fig. 56) is replete with classical overtones that resembled little else being done at the time. So potent an image was this work that *Two Self Portraits* appeared on the cover of the catalogue, which featured an introduction by Harold Rosenberg, for Johnson's February 1966 exhibition, *The Milford Paintings: 1964–65*, at the gallery. It is only in recent years that a new wave of artists has begun to approximate the brusque handling of paint and imagery so typically Johnson's.

An authentically robust artist, Johnson's contribution has a special meaning with regard to his contemporaries, whose art his own painting seems so little to resemble. A work of the mid-1960s, *Three Graces Blue* (fig. 57) resembles neither the cool disinterest of pop nor the nonfigurative abstract expressionism to which his painthandling would otherwise seem most easily reconcilable. His dealer understood the solid art historical foundations upon which his distortions depended and

urged the Johnsons to make the expensive trip to Europe to see a Vermeer show.[104]

Only the keenest insight into his paintings' intricacies would unite a sympathy for Vermeer with Johnson's stoutly energetic execution and subject matter.[105] A more recent work, *City Women* (fig. 58), is distinguished by Johnson's penchant for an expanded range of color and the modeling which that entails. The painter tried to extend the range of his concerns to a kind of monumentality independent of actual size, an endeavor that resembles, among modern artists, no one else as closely, or surprisingly, as Renoir. Whatever the humanistic content of his work with regard to the classical disposition of the human being amid turmoil, his dedication to the formal properties of paint prefigure much recent experimentation with slablike surfaces, while "his complete commitment to the figure would enlarge the scope of Abstract Expressionism, going beyond de Kooning's 'Women' and Pollock's late black and white figurative images."[106] Considering that Johnson first met Martha Jackson at her exhibition of de Kooning's work, this becomes an impressively fateful observation; the sensibility that brought him to the gallery as a spectator eventually united him with the history of that gallery.

Veteran sculptor Phillip Pavia is represented in the Martha Jackson Memorial Collection by two very dif-

44

Figure 57. Lester Johnson, *Three Graces Blue*, 1966 (cat. no. 81)

Figure 58. Lester Johnson,
City Women, 1973 (cat. no. 83)

Figure 59. Phillip Pavia, *Portrait Head of Martha Jackson*, 1971 (cat. no. 107)

ferent pieces that nevertheless spring from the same sensibility. Pavia's cast bronze portrait head of Martha Jackson (fig. 59) differs markedly from his blocky abstract marble pieces, of which the *Amazon on Horseback* (cat. no. 106) is a fine example. The wide swings in Pavia's approach indicate the latitude over which he has ranged. Some observers have been bewildered by these shifts; others, such as John Ashberry, found the sculptor's willingness to experiment heartening.

Phillip Pavia in an exhibition of recent marble sculptures showed again how exhilarating and horizon-expanding has been for him the return from bronze-casting to stone-carving. There was in the bronze work a strong Expressionists element which may have been due partly to the fact that bronze or plaster is shapeless before use and therefore responds all the more readily to the propositions of the sculptor. Marble, however, is already a form—blocks —before anybody touches it....[107]

Pavia sees himself as the practitioner of an art with a continuous tradition that reaches back to antiquity. He works only with marble from Italy, Greece, or Spain, which he selects for the distinctive coloring, texture and the individual markings of each block. His methods of working are archaic; there are easier ways to work stone than handcarving, handrubbing, and handpolishing each section. Especially since his work is nonobjective, and the spectator may associate such lavish attention with "old master" works of high realism, this labor seems eccentric, or perhaps obsessive. That lustrous marble skin attracts the eye to the refined treatment and niceties of Pavia's almost miniature art—indoor sculpture that contrasts with his plans for gargantuan outdoor pieces in stone. Pieces that never measure more than a couple of feet in diameter evoke through their purity of materials and design a perfectly rational architecture with the nostalgically beautiful decrepitude of Greek ruins. At once miniature (despite the weight of the stone), yet grand, the work seems midway between an ornamentally sized personal art and grand architectural planning. With the sculpture resting on a base or the floor plane, one looks down, into, and around such a work as *Amazon on Horseback*; yet, that supporting plane operates very much like a landscape surface, a surrogate for surrounding terrain. Our vision seems elevated, and we feel exalted observers of enormous size looking down on a new Stonehenge. There is a genuine consensus about just how successful *Amazon on Horseback* was at achieving its seemingly contradictory purposes; Pavia was represented by it on the announcement of his 1966 show at the gallery, and it was reproduced in an article about him the following year.

When Bob Thompson died at the age of twenty-nine, his work hung in few museums and in but a handful of private collections. Descended from American Indians, black slaves, and white farmers, Thompson was born in the segregated city of Louisville, Kentucky, in 1937. His father died in an automobile crash when Bob was thirteen, and his mother, a school teacher, saw medicine as her son's passport from prejudice. Instead of following this sensible maternal advice, young Thompson painted fiercely on any and every surface he could find or steal— including all the windowshades in his home. He studied at Boston University, at the University of Louisville, and met his first serious artists when, in Provincetown, Massachusetts, in the summer of 1958, he encountered Jack Tworkov (while fixing his roof) and Mark Rothko (when performing carpentry for him).

An ardent student, he copied endlessly from the old masters, especially Piero della Francesca, Masaccio, Raphael, and Breughel—all painters of vigor and clarity. A subsequent trip to Paris so overwhelmed him that he sketched incessantly. Everything he saw he synthesized, driven by an animating religious faith that allowed him to combine motifs and formal elements and unite them

Figure 60. Bob Thompson, *The Spinning, Spinning, Turning, Directing,* 1963 (cat. no. 125)

with his natural expressionism and vigorous color. However feverish that emotional drive became, manifested as a primitive personal iconography that welled up from dreams, Thompson never relinquished the mastery he inherited, or took, from the past. *The Spinning, Spinning, Turning, Directing* (fig. 60) combines personal nightmares (swooping birds in a powerful night wind) and figures adapted from the old masters. Thompson's forceful color was intense almost to the point of primitiveness. This precarious mixture—of unaltered dream/drug imagery, wild yet sophisticated compositions, balanced by saturated color—marked the distant horizons he wished to touch in his art.

A fellowship allowed him to continue his stay in Europe and he and his wife moved to Spain where, quitting drugs, he produced a prodigious amount of work. One of his works of that period, *Descent from the Cross* (fig. 61), borrows elements from Goya, particularly from the Spanish master's suite of etchings and aquatints *Los Caprichios.* Goya's works combined the nightmare world of folktales with an embittered political vision;

Thompson, citing such folktales *through* the art of Goya, reviews the stories that underlie Christianity, legends whose origins rest deep in the folkloric mind of the Mediterranean. Hard, saturated colors heighten the original horrific story of the crucified king/martyr, and the gracefully beautiful entourage of female attendants that had been assembled over centuries of retelling; Thompson, in the wake of Goya, reverted to the crudely superstitious, broken peasantry from whose midst a carpenter-messiah might arise. When Bob Thompson returned to the United States in the fall of 1963 the Martha Jackson Gallery exhibited some of his European paintings.

Morbidly haunted, Thompson expected to die young and likened himself to Baudelaire or Modigliani, who had destroyed themselves by work, drink, drugs, syphilis and the compulsions of high romanticism which propelled them toward self-extinction. He forced himself to go without sleep in orgies of work and painted as pursued by death. From such moments of terrible self-persecution came the wonderful large crayon drawing,

Figure 61. Bob Thompson, *Descent From the Cross,* 1963 (cat. no. 126)

Prayers in a Landscape (from Piero della Francesca's *The Legend of the Cross: Hercules Bringing the Cross to Jerusalem*) (fig. 62). His autumn 1965 exhibition at the gallery broke all attendance records. By the next year he was dead.

Meyer Schapiro's statement about Thompson's remarkable talent issues from a sensibility that bridges the very chasm Thompson had chosen to cross—the modern and the venerable.

> *Bob Thompson painted from the fullness of a warm heart. His canvas was open to daydreams and anxieties. It was an innocent soliloquy, without thought of an audience. The meanings were sometimes as obscure to himself as to others.*
>
> *He gave his strange images a rhapsodical hotness—fiery reds and blacks, sharp zigzags, sweeping curves and diagonals, beside the tender undulations of naked bodies. Made about color and rhythm and acutely attentive to the weight of tones and shapes, he was a natural artist, closer in spirit to the unlettered Negro musicians he loved than to the writers, in spite of what seems literary in his work. Yet his idols were the great masters: Piero della Francesca, Raphael, Poussin. Their serene order and breadth were often on his mind and led him in his last years to a more deliberate and tempered art.*
>
> *His death at 29 is a tragic loss. Painters with Thompson's vitality and understanding are extremely rare.*[108]

Despite her general preoccupation with abstract expressionism, Martha Jackson was closely associated with Thompson. In retrospect, we can see how prescient a choice this partnership was, especially when reviewing criticism of Thompson's work from the twilight of postwar abstraction's reign.

> *That he is not generally well-known has much to do with the fact that his chosen style—figurative Expressionism—was and remains perhaps the most implacably unfashionable of currently vital modes in American painting....It is also rather painful to reflect (let's face it) that he had to be dead to receive his due. Were he inconveniently still alive, pressing the claims of his preposterous style, he could hardly expect so handsome a reward....*[109]

Neither figurative nor abstract, at the beginning of the 1960s, Julian Stanczak worked completely outside public recognition to experiment with a fallow area of artistic theory. It is hard to reconstruct how aberrant *Determinative Focus* (fig. 63) seemed to the general public at the time. For those who derided abstract expressionism, such a painting—consisting of nothing but black and white lines—seemed to lack even the verve and irritating gusto of that brash style. If the techniques that typified abstract expressionism lacked authority (recalling phrases like "My kid could do it"), what would one make of this painting done, apparently, with a ruler and monochromatic colors. If schooled manual dexterity of the kind measured by academic standards was hard to locate in abstract expressionism, it was patently and utterly nonexistent in Stanczak's paintings.

Julian Stanczak's work was not prominently placed before the public until he began to work with Martha Jackson. He was born in Poland and had studied in Uganda, London, and at the Cleveland Institute of Art before receiving his M.F.A. from Yale University where Josef Albers and Marca-Relli presided. Before his solo show in New York he had hardly exhibited. Martha Jackson first saw Stanczak's work at the Dayton Art Institute in the spring of 1964, and, shortly thereafter, invited him to mount a solo exhibition at her gallery. Stanczak remembers that

> *When I came to the opening in New York, I found the sign in her window:*
>
> OPTICAL PAINTINGS
>
> *which made me quite mad. Why say "visual" twice?! So I stormed to her office, "Martha, take this sign off! My paintings deal with select visual energy—optical means trickery!" She listened, put her hand on my shoulder to calm me down, and said, "This is only something for the critics to chew on." She would not budge. I enjoyed her conviction, but at the same time remained perturbed about the term.*
>
> *That evening I went to see Josef Albers to invite him to come to my show. I found him on his porch in Orange with the New York Times on his lap waiting. The first thing he said, pounding his finger into the*

Figure 62. Bob Thompson, *Prayers in a Landscape* (from Piero della Francesca's *The Legend of the Cross: Hercules Bringing the Cross to Jerusalem*), 1966 (cat. no. 127)

paper was, "Julian, your obligation is to correct this!" The announcement in the paper said,

JULIAN STANCZAK—OPTICAL PAINTINGS

I went back to Martha; Martha would not change her mind. Later Time *and* Life *and Richard Borgzinner were responsible for the term Op Art.*[110]

Thus, in reviews of Stanczak's work the term op art was born, midwifed by Martha Jackson. Stanczak's works have ranged from the rigorous to the playful to the thoughtful pieces such as *Rectangular Fold in Yellow* (fig. 64), which is the clear descendent of Alber's monochromatic experimental pieces that established complex planar twists through descriptive perspective. The painting's spaces are unlike the volumes we traverse as we move through the world, nor is it the ballet-like space created by expressionist brushwork, with its implications of titanic scale. Rather this is a calm mental space, impossible to invade by gesture or cast shadows. Surprisingly, given the aesthetic climate of the times, his work found a ready audience.

Stanczak recalls a conversation with Martha Jackson during his first exhibition in New York:

"Look Julian, you drew people in minks and business suits! Come to some of our other openings—the people will have straw between their toes." I was delighted. The reaction of the public to my exhibition was very good. I give Martha credit for being very perceptive, not only about my work, but about the leading role she played in other movements. She would always be one of the first to recognize, promote, and time the appearance of a particular visual form. She said to me once, "My objective for a gallery is to create life out of the young artist's dreams and ideas…." and she succeeded well in this endeavor.[111]

The double canvas *Majestic* (fig. 65), which is full of rich color, seems stately, although one is at a loss to say

Figure 63. Julian Stanczak, *Determinative Focus*, 1962 (cat. no. 117)

just how this effect was achieved. In fact, Stanczak was one of the few painters using these rigorous means who could transcend technical aspects to arrive at some manner of expression. In time his pieces evolved from irregular and nervous patterns to regular and predictable rhythms. His work traversed the distance between novelty in manipulating the retinal impression to discovering this same channel as an expressive means.

...I remember when Martha scheduled me for another one-man show I was perturbed about the frequency and whether I could fulfill the need for good new work. So I expressed my worries to Martha. She pretended not to listen. Then she turned around and asked me point blank: "How many paintings do you paint a year!" I said, twenty-five, roughly and her answer to that was, "What! twenty-five. A hundred and twenty-five!" I was frustrated and walked through the park; it was difficult to paint twenty-five paintings you are proud of. But I saw her reasoning. She would purposely drive young artists to the brim, to

the threshold, which she believed young people need in order to explore all the possible thoughts and make them become reality, to be executed so they could clarify their dreams and condition themselves to a creative process which embraces every hour of living. It was not the number of paintings Martha was interested in. Martha was not only a connoisseur and a dealer, she was also an educator to the young artist.[112]

In retrospect, it seems astonishing that through the instrument of her *New Forms* shows and her presentation of Stanczak, Martha Jackson found herself in the vanguard of both pop and op art.

Disregarding the idea of a consistent and comprehensible image for the gallery, Martha Jackson began showing the largely figurative paintings of Emilio Cruz. Born in New York, Cruz studied at the Art Students League with Edwin Dickinson, Frank J. Reilly, and George Grosz. Cruz had shown in Provincetown as well as the Zabriskie Gallery before joining Martha Jackson.

Figure 64. Julian Stanczak, *Rectangular Fold in Yellow*, 1971 (cat. no. 120)

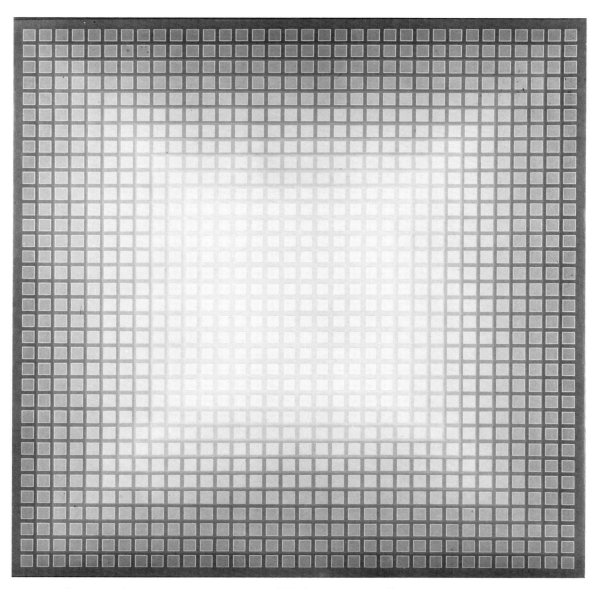

Figure 65. Julian Stanczak, *Majestic* (two canvases, red and blue), 1978 (cat. no. 123)

Figure 66. Emilio Cruz, *Figurative Composition #7*, 1965 (cat. no. 24)

Figure 67. Emilio Cruz, *The Dance*, 1962, oil on paper mounted on fiberboard, 21⅞ x 30⅝ in. (55.5 x 77.8 cm.). National Museum of American Art, Smithsonian Institution, Washington, D.C. Gift of Virginia Zabriskie.

I received a letter from Martha Jackson inviting me to exhibit, while I was in Rome; you can't imagine the excitement....Martha Jackson was a woman of outstanding character that I have always been fully aware of. Her dignity went far beyond her position as an outstanding N.Y. art dealer. She was a woman who knew no prejudice at a time when racism in the art world would have gone unnoticed. She gave opportunity based on merit or perhaps magic, what reached inside of her and unravelled her inner core. Even style created no limitation, for she did not pursue fashion and the consequence of that fashion pursued her. Her love of art reflected her belief in truth. I write these things now after many years have passed and a multitude of hard lessons learned.[113]

His early work showed a brilliantly joyous fauvism as well as distorted figures that recalled darkly brooding German expressionism. Like Bob Thompson, another brillant young black painter, Cruz seems to have been influenced by Jan Müller. A strong example of his painting, *Figurative Composition #7* (fig. 66), hints at the range of colors and treatments to which the figure could be put. *The Dance* (fig. 67), is noticeably different—less aggressive, far looser in the application of paint and of a grayer tonality. A comparison of the two shows the markedly geometric penchant that appears in the latter work, and eventually that urge toward a formal orderliness prevailed. For a time Cruz abandoned the figure (*Angola's Dreams Grasp Finger Tips*, cat. no. 25) only to return to it with renewed strength. Sooner or later just about every possibility of painthandling came under his purview as

> *a virtual slang of paintsmanship, Cruz indulges the dynamics of gesture—brash impasto smears, squirted squiggles, runny stains—within a structural (and conceptual) straightjacket of geometric contours.*[114]

An odd form of "cool" portraiture practiced by Marisol (Escobar) resembles work done by no other artist, although it draws on both the traditions of painting and sculpture. A form of assemblage that unites carved and painted wooden elements, no technique is alien to her art which transforms ready-made, store-bought materials. At heart a sort of satire, her work does not satirize art but rather Marisol's subjects, and to the degree that her visually pleasant pieces do not critique the assumptions of art itself, they are not a form of pop. Marisol's production represents an idiosyncratic body of work whose acceptance seemed to depend on the historical appearance of pop at the same time.

Among the most celebrated of her pieces is *Charles DeGaulle* (cat. no. 29). The monumental construction was featured in *Look* magazine and in Britain's *Daily Telegraph Magazine*. In the course of these articles the artist stated some of her intentions for this piece: "It isn't really a caricature at all, is it? I found myself putting together a rather straightforward likeness of DeGaulle." The sculpture stands on a wheeled carriage and rears up nine feet high. Her first thoughts for the piece's base were somewhat derisively funny; for two days she worked on two wooden horses' rumps irreverently framing a woman's buttocks, but this was never used because "it didn't look right." Typical of her willingness to combine any technique with her self-taught carpentry is the rendition of DeGaulle's eyes and jowls that are drawn in pencil, and not carved. The small hand atop the torso is a characteristically odd touch—it was cast from Marisol's own hand and wears her signet ring. In spite of this, Marisol remarked that "DeGaulle is so funny, I copied him almost exactly."[115]

Of Venezuelan family, European upbringing, and

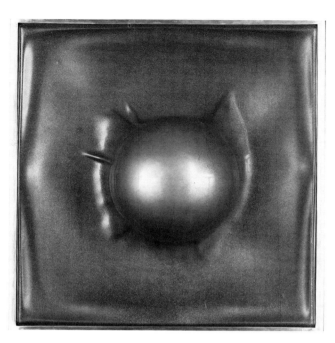

Figure 68. Ed McGowin, *LOS-1*, 1966, vacuum-formed plastic, 23¾ x 22⅝ x 10 in. (60.3 x 57.5 x 25.5 cm.). National Museum of American Art, Smithsonian Institution, Washington, D.C. Gift of James M. Younger.

American schooling, Marisol considers herself an American and she has been woven into the history of modern art mainly as an American player. Her relationship with the Martha Jackson Gallery never became firmly established by contract, and she never had a solo show at the gallery.

Ed McGowin arrived in Washington, D.C., in 1961 for a year's stay as a Congressional page. What he learned of art he discovered from magazine pieces about Morris Louis and Kenneth Noland. He soon met Howard Mehring, another of the key figures in the Washington Color movement, who impressed McGowin with the all-over patterns of his delicately colored stain paintings. By the next year the Corcoran Gallery of Art was showing McGowin's experimental works, small paintings with variously shaped holes to which were affixed clear windows. He had effectively leap-frogged his artistic education and propelled himself into the avant-garde, showing at Washington art galleries and gaining a position of prominence as he began vacu-forming plastic into works that were neither paintings nor sculptures, but occupied a position midway between each realm (fig. 68).

Ed McGowin's work came to Martha Jackson's attention when she saw his pieces in the Whitney Museum Annual in 1966. As McGowin recalls,

> *In the late 1960s, the anything-goes-period, I was investigating new materials such as plexiglass-vacuum-forming and I think that is what interested Martha about my work. The time was so volatile, that if something new appeared on the market, before it could be distributed,*

Figure 69. Ed McGowin, *Three Locked Pyramids*, 1967 (cat. no. 100)

artists would snap it up and somehow co-opt it into their image.[116]

A charcoal drawing *Three Locked Pyramids* (fig. 69) is a study for one of his formed plastic works. The drawing displays a sensuous play of moving surface tones to suggest something of the shimmering quality of the plastic. Both the drawing and the sculptural pieces that followed are worked with an attentiveness that belies the care-free moment through which the artist lived.

While the mechanical aspects of the vacu-forming process appealed to McGowin, in fact, its potential to extend the possibilities of abstract expressionism attracted him to the technique, and attracted Martha Jackson to McGowin. Mounting his works, so different from the physical demands exacted by paintings, tested the patience and commitment of the dealer as she prepared for McGowin's first one-man show in New York.

I had made a number of requests regarding how the pieces would be installed on the wall. Martha had objected to the techniques, explaining that it would create a lot of damage to an old plaster wall that was difficult to repair. I insisted and eventually she agreed to let me do what I wanted. Later, when we were sitting in the gallery, looking at the exhibition before the opening (after I had mangled her

walls considerably), she was talking very quietly about how the work looked and what she thought about the exhibition. It was a particularly perceptive and sensitive conversation on her part. At some point, I interrupted her and asked how much money she thought I would make, demanding to know if she thought I would sell out the show. I think at that point she finally realized what a bumpkin she was dealing with. She turned to me and very pointedly said, "I don't think you understand—this first show is charity."[117]

Her support of artists extended to other regional reputations, such as Stanley Dean Edwards who met Martha Jackson when he was a twenty-one-year-old celebrity in the Chicago art world. Jackson visited his gallery in Chicago and immediately bought three pictures from his show (among them *Baby in an Altar No. IV*, cat. no. 28). Following an initial success, backed by Jackson and her gallery, Edwards moved to New York in 1967. For him, the

…following years were to be ones filled with a kind of sad madness. I, like many around me, merged with the insanity of the 60's. We lived in a kind of intense unreality. Paintings painted only to be lost or destroyed along with friends and ideals. In 1970 I moved back to my home

*and in the years since I have thought often of those early
60s days of Martha, her gallery, and the talk we had about
a one man show that was never to be. I realize now that
she knew what that kind of exposure would do to me
rather than for me....Of course I was only one of the
many whose life she touched and that touch, however
brief, was profound.*[118]

More typical of the works for which the gallery was
best known are the bright, airy, and frankly abstract
expressionist paintings of Joan Mitchell, a Chicagoan by
birth, who, after graduating from Smith College,
returned to the Art Institute of Chicago (B.F.A. 1947).
Later she earned an M.F.A. from New York University,
did further study at Columbia University, and now lives
and works in Europe.

To Harold Rosenberg, Mitchell's world was circum-
scribed by the tenets of abstract expressionism: "her
compositions revel in the liberationist draftsmanship
and paint handling developed by postwar American
abstract art."[119] Indeed, in the early 1950s, painting in a
studio on St. Marks Place, she attended meetings of the
artists' club and, along with the other abstract expressionists, favored the Cedar Tavern as a meeting place.
Yet for certain viewers her works did not fall neatly into
a category or type: "Joan Mitchell should ... be seen first
as a traditional artist and as an independent, not as a
member of a specific movement or of a generation. The
major interest is landscape as an expression in itself and
simultaneously, as an expression of herself."[120] Despite
such careful distinctions introduced into the history of
the period—divisions that perhaps identify the procliv-
ties of the author more than the painter—she participated in the full life of the artistic community in New
York at that time, her career describing the trajectory of
a successful abstract expressionist.

In 1951 she participated in the Ninth Street *Show*,
organized with the help of Leo Castelli, and had her first
solo exhibition at the New Gallery before beginning to
divide her time between France and New York. Her
affiliation with the Martha Jackson Gallery came com-
paratively late in her career when she was already an
established artist of some repute. But once that relationship was forged, it remained relatively stable. If some of
the New York School artists initiated paintings with a
scrawled phrase, an anatomical citation, or some con-
figuration drawn from autobiographical materials, Mitchell's method of working was not so very different. The
open network of brush strokes that describes *My Landscape II* (fig. 70) is composed of a loose array that combines into a generous vista. This open use of liquid paint
that freely runs down the canvas is reminiscent of
Gorky's usage, which he borrowed from Picasso. Eventually this sort of painting gave way to another vision of
work, more close-up and offering less depth within the
picture. Of this transition James Harithas remarked
that, "thematically she has gradually changed her paint-

Figure 70. Joan Mitchell, *My Landscape II*, 1967 (cat. no. 102)

ings, from generalized landscapes in the earlier works, to
sunflowers in the late 1960s, and to the specific landscapes, wet with light, in which she lives."[121] The Martha
Jackson Memorial Collection contains one of these later
paintings, *Sunflower III* (fig. 71), as bright and open a
work as Mitchell has every produced. The brushwork
seems to dance across the surface of the picture as if the
paint were not, finally, limning anything in particular,
yet, upon examination, the whole comes together to
form a singularly lyrical view.

Her luminous painting is marked by more variety of
intense hues than is typical of the other abstract expressionists, and a delicate, fastidious touch that is not the
universal attribute of her generation's energetic painting. Irving Sandler commented that

*the prevalence of swift, arcing lines makes Mitchell's pic-
tures appear lyrical in a way that de Kooning's, especially,
and Kline's do not although like theirs, hers were often
characterized as aggressive, even violent.*[122]

Harold Rosenberg responded that "Mitchell has
absorbed the physicality of Action painting—the element of dance in it."[123]

Subsequent history has shown the remarkable underlying continuity of Martha Jackson's selections. In a

Figure 71. Joan Mitchell, *Sunflower III*, 1969 (cat. no. 103)

1984 review of a Norman Bluhm exhibition, a critic pointed out that his show,

> ...remarkable enough in itself, paves the way for another event of equal importance...an exhibition...which focuses on Bluhm, Michael Goldberg, Grace Hartigan, Al Held, Al Leslie, and Joan Mitchell as they were in the 1950s.
>
> Apart from setting Bluhm in context the...[hypothetical] exhibition may retrieve the decade from the semi-limbo it's been consigned to; it could rescue the artists (all born between 1920 and 1927) from the makeshift catagory of "second generation" Abstract Expressionism. The term, chronologically useful though it is, smacks a bit of movies, such as "Rocky II," that seek to repeat the success of their blockbuster predecessors. That subsequent exponents of Abstract Expressionism haven't been tagged "third generation" is doubtless because of the drastic decline in the mode's box office in the 1960s.[124]

Falling in the shadow of their brilliant predecessors this "second generation" was forced to win anew territory that had been gained as high ground once before.

One of the artists who most forcefully came to her attention presented himself in an audacious meeting in October 1968. Dennis Byng recalls:

> [I] brought three of my polished lucite sculptures into the gallery without an appointment and placed them on the desk of the receptionist, this, of course, being strictly against gallery rules. The woman at the receptionist desk at that moment happened to be Martha Jackson's personal secretary. She said, "It's a shame Martha can't see these, but I'm sure you understand the gallery procedures of first getting slides of the artist's work." At that very moment the phone rang and Martha Jackson herself came down the stairs to accept the phone call. She was talking to her client, at the same time she was berating me, her private secretary, and the sculpture. As she talked on she started peeking around viewing the sculptures from different angles and touching and feeling them. By the time her conversation was over she was a bit intrigued with the pieces, had a smile on her face, and wanted to meet me.[125]

The works to which Jackson took such an instant liking were cast acrylic-lucite sculptures, an extremely difficult medium in which to work—so imperious that few modern artist have done significant work with this material, although it is the quintessential product of our times. A small work like *Column with Orange, Blue, Green Diagonals* (fig. 72) tests the limits of a formal rigor that bordered on an industrial look. Only a meticulous technical procedure allows Byng to work as flawlessly as he does, and it was the precision of his work that attracted Jackson. His transition from intruder to colleague came quickly.

 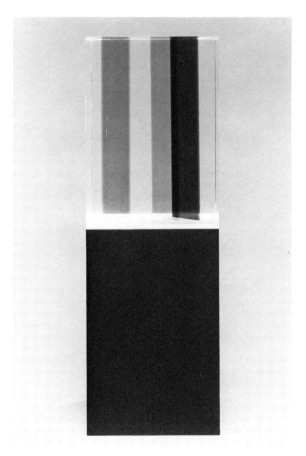

Figure 72. Dennis Byng, *Column with Orange, Blue, Green Diagonals*, 1969 (cat. no. 16)

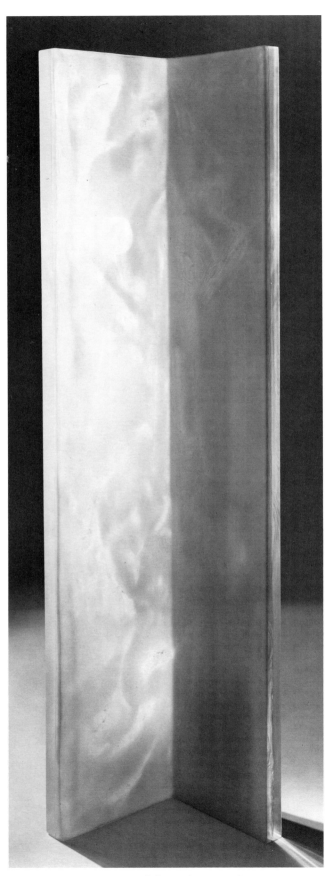

Figure 73. Dennis Byng, Untitled, 1976 (cat. no. 17)

The smaller pieces gave way to increasingly larger works like an untitled piece (fig. 73) that marked successive stages of his mastery of his materials. The notices of that first show confirmed Jackson's belief in the young artist. One reviewer exulted that, "His somewhat Constructivist color and form, transposed to a sculptural format, are a gentle knockout. His rectangular, laminated modules of bright color are suspended in transparent plexiglass columns, but are kept kinetic through some sorcery which allows them to splay out handsomely according to the angle of the eye."[127] Another critic wrote:

> *To the eye, plexiglass is so diaphanous as to be invisible; it is literally nothing, in formal terms pure volume. But to the touch it is opaque, impenetrable; in formal terms, it is mass. As "solid void," then, plexiglass teaches the senses to distrust each other, and in the mild bafflement and wonder which results lies some of the charm of Dennis Byng's work....*
>
> *They are part of an ascetic vocabulary familiar since De Stijl—pure geometric form and a limited number of hues that never vary. But of these rigid elements Byng makes rich use....Edge on, they are slim volumes that float; turned slightly, their edges blur and they become areas; turned still more they begin to dye the plexiglass behind them and their effect is three-dimensional again. Also, as the slabs are translucent, all these effects are additive, color on color....Byng is a fine artist. With straight lines and right angles he coolly makes geometry create its gentlest adversary—flowers.*[128]

Like Claire Falkenstein, Byng's work extended constructivist thinking with uncharacteristic materials. Each contrasted volume with mass—Falkenstein with actual volumes that contained mainly open space, Byng with an external space envelope and a fictive interior scale. Falkenstein colored her spaces with the fused glass that she included in her works while Byng made color an essential ingredient in his constructed spaces and made that color the very identity of those zones. These two artists shared a fundamental sensibility with Julian Stanczak as well—particularly in his later works in which an optical space is created unrelated to perspective or volume; the three artists would have been surprised to learn they shared a common urge, for their work appears so vastly different each from the other, but Martha Jackson united them within the embrace of her gallery.

Eventually Byng synthesized the transparency of his earliest pieces with the richly dyed colors of his denser works so that he could control every range of hue and intensity from the faintest to most intense; he mastered color values from light to dark, all along a keyboard of possibilities that included both clear plastic and opaque zones within the works—such as in his *77A AA* (fig. 74). In Byng's work, somewhat surprisingly, location became color in a way that approaches the color space of Morris Louis (and subsequent color field painters, like Olitski or Poons). Unnoticed, Martha Jackson's taste presented a continuity that united her gallery artists in a program that they themselves might have endorsed, had anyone been aware of its existence.

With her son, David Anderson, Jackson exhibited many prominent Europeans, including Henry Moore, Antoni Tapies, Lucio Fontana, Gio Pomodoro, Karel Appel, and Lynn Chadwick. To further the artistic commerce and dialogue as well as the availability of European artists for the New York gallery, David Anderson maintained his own gallery in Paris for a few years. Throughout this period Anderson collaborated with Jackson on numerous exhibitions and projects. Then, Martha Jackson died suddenly on July 4, 1969, apparently of a massive cerebral hemorrhage while swimming in the pool at her summer home in Los Angeles. She was buried in her native city of Buffalo.

At her death David Anderson succeeded his mother as president of the gallery. His stewardship was neither quiescent nor conservative. He had never thought to use the gallery as a museum to preserve Martha Jackson's taste; instead he wanted to advance her proposition that one ought actively to engage in fervent examination of one's times. As she had, Anderson continued to seek what was new and personally attractive, regardless of how much or how little attention had previously been paid to the artists.

In October 1969 the gallery showed the works of Sam Richardson whose pieces had appeared in the Whitney Museum's 1968 Sculpture Annual, but whose first one-man show in the East was at the Martha Jackson Gallery. Until that time he was known almost exclusively in his native California. Richardson met Martha Jackson just weeks before she died, and his recollections of her are, inevitably, colored by the hindsight that he was the last artist she was to bring into her gallery.

...I was working in my converted garage in San Jose which is about fifty miles south of San Francisco—not exactly on the beaten path for one of the country's major and most respected art dealers. But that, of course, was Martha's gift to the very end of her life: that vital interest and energy in finding the artist and the work—wherever that pursuit might take her. After all the years of her

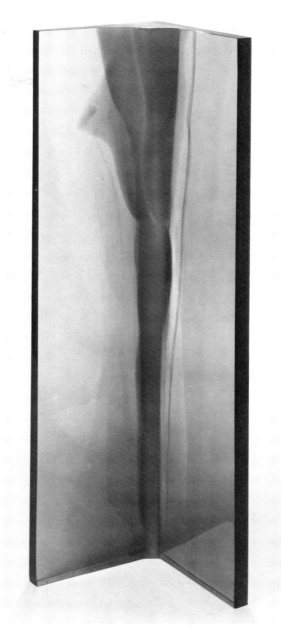

Figure 74. Dennis Byng, *77A AA*, 1977 (cat. no. 18)

remarkable career she had not become bored or comfortable or satisfied to let it come to her—she was, I think, enjoying that pursuit—the pleasure and excitement of the hunt, to the very last days of her life.

Her legacy to me—beyond the support of the gallery's exhibition of my work—was the profound encouragement that her interest in my work gave to me at a crucial point in my development as an artist. The spirit of that encouragement, and the examples of her curiosity, energy, and commitment to risk in the search for excellence are still with me.[129]

A work that appeared in his first show at the gallery and carried one of Richardson's typically precise titles

Figure 75. Sam Richardson, *A Very Thick Summer Overcast Extending Inland Near Antioch, California*, 1969 (cat. no. 108)

Figure 76. *A Very Thick Summer Overcast Extending Inland Near Antioch, California* (detail)

was *A Very Thick Summer Overcast Extending Inland Near Antioch, California* (figs. 75 and 76). To say that the sculpture "depicts" the situation described in its title diminishes the quality of what has been called his "sculpture-scapes."[130] This work is something of a triumph. At least three, or more, positions are required to figure out the basic disposition of the forms and how they communicate the basic air-to-ground relationship. If certain modernist sculpture (starting with Giacometti's plazas and squares) analogized the sculptural substrate to landscape, Richardson analogized the land to sculpture. Rather than suggest tiny fragments of actual terrain he miniaturized the land to reveal its sculptural possibilities. The initial impression made by Richard-

son's pieces is quite direct, and one would not be hard pressed to convey a superficial sense of what they depict. One reviewer issued a terse summary about the composition of Richardson's pieces in his first solo exhibition in New York.

Mountains and lakes and oceans are translated into plastic, reduced in size to a birds-eye-view scale and then lifted out of the terrain in box-like sections and installed on plexiglass pedestals. With titles that denote specific place and specific time....[131]

Starting with a plywood box, Richardson constructs the contours of the land with polyurethane foam or molds formations of the terrain he wishes to portray. Covered with fiberglass, the land is sanded to the desired smoothness, and into the hollows, valleys, and stream beds are fitted clear lakes and blue streams cast in polyester resin. Nitro-cellulose lacquers are sprayed on layer after layer, giving a matte finish to the colors that identify the climate (sun-drenched or gloomy), the time of day (twilight or high noon), or seasons. All of these techniques combine to render a hyper-real, though Lil-liputian, landscape that compresses a specific moment and poetic situation. The landscape is "edited" in various ways as different sorts of cross sections are made in the land. A narrow dissection, a strip through a complex ecology, characterizes *It's a Cool October Evening with a Little Lake at the Base of that Hill* (fig. 77). In this piece, geology and hydrology are brought into play to a greater degree than in other of Richardson's works in which meteorology controls the drama. Here a section of the land, seemingly to the center of the earth, makes us aware of the depth that lies beneath our feet as we tread the surface—a realization hard to communicate through other formal means.

Like Byng, Richardson used a highly complex modern technology to create a fictive space; unlike Byng, his space mirrored the natural landscape to give scale to the experience involved. Both artists relied on a palette of meltingly beautiful colors and shimmering rays of light, but each employed these qualities for effects that are so opposed as to constitute a dialogue. Unknown to each other, the two sculptors seemed to be asking similar questions and arriving at very different answers.

Richardson's works imply a host of associations having to do with his treatment of space and its reduction—his sources are obvious, his references clear, as opposed to the more hermetically mysterious miniaturist, Joseph Cornell, for example.

> *Richardson was interested in voluntary self-exclusion. There was no way to enter the opaque space of his "sculpture-scapes." When I disassembled one of them I experienced its components—air, earth and water—as identical in substance....I was excluded, referred back to the way a large natural landscape excludes the viewer if he restricts himself to looking. Then too air, earth and water are identical, having no substance, only appearance.*[132]

This experience is only possible because Richardson's pieces can be dismantled, element by element, inviting the viewer to separate water from land, airscape from landscape, and stream from its bed. To think of the vista as more-or-less interchangeable volumes transforms the spectacle from anything but sculptural consideration. Surprisingly, this quality of "opticality"—color and form without assignable volume—seems to contradict the very idea of sculpture, certainly sculpture that can be held in the hand. In contrast, works of extremely large size, works that challenged and addressed nature on its own terms, were just becoming aesthetically viable—even though they had been proposed for generations

Figure 77. Sam Richardson, *It's a Cool October Evening with a Little Lake at the Base of that Hill,* 1969 (cat. no. 109)

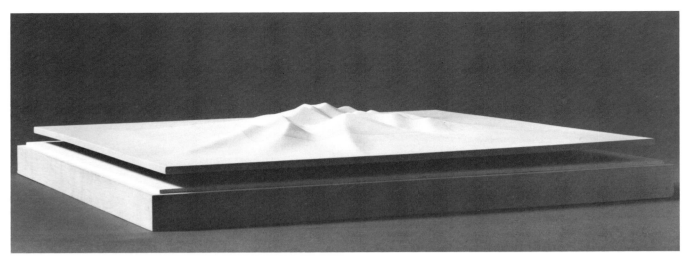

Figure 78. Sam Richardson, *Sierra Snow: Sunrise on East Face*, 1974 (cat. no. 112)

(and had many antecedents in titanic constructions like the Pyramids). It was clear that Richardson's works stood in some subtle opposition to "earthworks" and major excavation pieces, although both required the viewer to address the experiences of viewing the landscape in a theatrical framework.

> The difference between Sam Richardson's little plastic "earth works" and Robert Smithson's big real earth works is something like the difference between a person's having artistic talent and a person's having wealth: they both mean power, but there is the matter of scale.... watching the film of the Salt Lake [Great Spiral] jetty as seen from a helicopter a million miles away one got the same sort of marvellous feeling one experienced standing ever so slightly above one of Sam Richardson's plastic islands, that one was basking in the presence of some meat-headed fantasy that had been correctly and rigorously indulged.[133]

Surprisingly, for works that appear toylike, Richardson's sculptures recapitulate the romanticism of the American space that enthralled our artists from the first settlers through Cole, Church, Bierstadt, and Moran. This could not be more clearly stated than in an example *Sierra Snow: Sunrise on East Face,* (fig. 78). Once again, Americans were invited to ask themselves in what authority and with what sensations they occupied this land.

An alternately heroic and miserable figure, Jochen Seidel was born on April Fool's Day (which he featured in many of his late works) in Germany, a member of the "white generation," who (like Gunter Grass, for example, who was a friend) grew up under Hitler. In a internal Brown Shirt purge, Seidel's father was murdered (in such a way that his death would resemble a suicide), and in the late 1930s Seidel was drafted into the Hitler youth movement, graduated from gymnasium, and conscripted into the German army. During the war he was taken prisoner by the Russians, then the British, only to find himself in the East after Germany's surrender. He became a leading Soviet practitioner of the heavy-handed style of approved social realism. In 1953 he managed to escape both its leaden art and the Russian occupation, making his way to West Berlin, where he began to practice his equally successful but authentic abstract expressionism. Seidel was soon as well received in his new career as he had been in the feigned Soviet style he had been forced to practice. His work was shown throughout Europe, South America, and the United States. He participated in the 1961 Carnegie International and, the following year, was brought to this country to teach at Fairleigh Dickenson University.

In a relatively short time he had gone from being a Soviet "star" to a German celebrity and the first hope of its postwar painting to an unknown in New York—where he felt that his art would continue to grow. In New York he was highly respected by both dealers and his fellow artists, but Seidel was an exceedingly difficult person—a manic depressive who had failed in two marriages and committed suicide in the summer of 1971. Because of his unpredictable nature, few dealers wished to represent him; paradoxically, his death ushered in a new appreciation of his works.

Only David Anderson, of the many New Yorkers who had admired Seidel's work, stepped forward to represent him, and his confidence has been rewarded as Seidel's reputation grows more lustrous on both sides of the Atlantic—although Europeans are still better disposed to this artist who worked so hard to become an *American* painter. Indeed, the appreciation of Seidel's work involves the same historical perspective as must be brought to bear when viewing Morandi (who had to "re-invent" Cézanne), or DeStäel (who had to "re-invent" the fauves). If one looks for novelty in Seidel's work, the

Figure 79. Jochen Seidel, *Mind Your Train Depository*, ca. 1963-67 (cat. no. 115)

Figure 80. Jochen Seidel, *Untitled (Appletree Song)*, 1965, acrylic on canvas, 81¼ x 65½ in. (206.5 x 166.1 cm.). National Museum of American Art, Smithsonian Institution, Washington, D.C. Gift of Jo Roman.

search will be mostly unrewarded; he recapitulated the major themes of abstract expressionism. To this degree he does not belong to any "second generation" because he did not inherit his art's terms but rather sought again the original impetus to abstraction.

> *Seidel was in the wrong place at the wrong time. He gravitated to New York to be at the nerve center of the art world, but...the predominant styles of the 1960s...were cool, clean and rational in conception. Seidel's work is distinctly European, with its roots in Expressionism and Surrealism. A linear emphasis infuses the forms with both grace and agitation. The looping arabesques constantly shift direction and the shapes they define interlock...the full effect is of energy roped into place by its own nervousness....Often the pictures include written inscriptions in fluid letters....One senses the automatism of Miró's and Masson's Surrealism and the existential vigor, hovering between anguish and merriment, of the COBRA painters.[134]*

The vigor and the tortured self-questioning that brought him to a fusion of calligraphy, painting, and drawing appear in *Mind Your Train Depository* (fig. 79), which is a direct descendent not only of Goldberg's use of letters but also of the enormous spaces of Caspar David Friedrich. In such work the landscape does not whisper its burden of meaning but screams it. Unlike Lester John-

son's use of script, Seidel's epigraphy yields massively important personal assertions rather than another mere layer of formal contribution. Puns of a high order, sometimes in more than one language, reveal the multiplex thinking and invention that characterized his production. In a slippery transformation, the forms exchanged shapes and identities; words took on the coloring and associations of neighboring discursive signs; all was provisional, all meanings retreated to evermore distant certitude to produce a nervous, brilliant entry to the mind itself—the actual subject of Seidel's works despite the putative subject matter of any given one. In his paintings (*Untitled: Appletree Song*, fig. 80) the transformation of his shapes is carried even further, making the original calligraphy—where it is present—wholly illegible as language, but imperceptibly merged with the formal language of the work.

The companion to *Mind Your Train Depository*, *Train Your Mind* (fig. 81), is an equally complex piece. It is also partly a discursive (if semi-deranged) letter—part calligraphy, part painting—that possesses and opens an inner terrain which the spectator may wander, halting now and again to read words that make up forms, much as a hiker pauses to examine geology. That Seidel employed an improvisatory manner to create these works might categorize him as an action painter, but Seidel worked methodically and developed his pieces in long series until he became sufficiently adroit at executing his themes, fully understanding the properties of his shapes, colors, and letters.

That Seidel's art was hermetic was perhaps as much the result of his pathology as his stylistic ambitions. The final result of his furious efforts and exhausted life are works whose complex interchange of symbols begins with simple word play or witty exchange of shapes and recedes—faster than the balanced mind can keep up—into evermore distant areas of association and violent poetry.

Anderson expanded the gallery's activities and, to augment the East Side building, added another location that eventually supplanted the first. In March 1975 he inaugurated an enormous new space at 521 West 57th Street; the openness of this huge industrial building (converted for the gallery's uses) had 200 running feet of space and promised wonderful possibilities for sculpture installations. In addition to extending the public exhibition spaces of the older, domestically scaled East Side gallery, the West Side facility was to function as an area for press previews and private viewings for client presentations. Reporters commented upon the novelty of the Martha Jackson West location and the continuity of the gallery's mission.

> *Despite the 57th Street address, the warehouse is no stone's throw from Marlborough [Gallery], or [Sidney] Janis [Gallery]. On the northern edge of the working-class Hell's Kitchen area, it is a good half-mile west of the midtown*

gallery row, and far closer to the piers and industrial buildings of the waterfront....Anderson and his associates were undaunted by the thought of opening up a home away from home in Siberia. SoHo, after all, had been terra incognita only a few years back....They want to present the work to the public at eminently reasonable prices, establishing a market for new artists during a time of scarce money. The chief beneficiaries of this policy will be the artists themselves. Of course the Martha Jackson Gallery stands only to gain prestige and capital should the buying public not prove overly timid or fickle, but there is certainly something symbiotic in the open, gracious relationship the M[artha] J[ackson] W[est] intends to maintain with its artists.[135]

The relationship of the dealer and his artists that typified Martha Jackson's practices was fading, along with the narrow but intense audience for the work. Years after she died Norman Bluhm observed that

Most of them [dealers] know nothing about art, they just have a certain style, "politesse." By accepting the rule of the dealer the artist destroys himself, better than anyone else could. New York now means this destructive merchandising of art.[136]

Elaine Kurtz was one of those who showed in this new space. Anderson found her work appealing and decided to show her paintings in New York. In a letter to Kurtz dated April 1977, he divulged his ambitions for the gallery in its new location.

I must tell you that I am engaged in a personal search, of which West 57th Street is the physical manifestation, to break the mold of established Gallery activities. Over 20 years ago my mother pioneered with contracts for unknown contemporary artists, and by accepting major risks (or so they seemed at the time) helped enormously to create a public for contemporary art. The pattern she established is now followed by 800 galleries, some of whom do it better, some do it worse....Sure it is great to have 800 one-man shows a month for the delectation of New York's lonely few remaining serious art interests. But the old ways are bankrupt right now, the costs of "prestige" have overrun the local market. Artists cannot be treated like farmers, expected to supply their art at a tiny fraction of the public price, in order to support an extravagant, and very inefficient system of public exposure.[137]

Anderson visited Kurtz's Washington, D.C., studio and quickly discovered her strongest work, divining in her rigorous painting a pattern of promise; he organized a solo exhibition for the next fall. In preparation for her exposure to the New York audience the gallery prepared a catalogue, a postcard announcement, advertising, and an opening reception. The expenses for this investment would not have been covered even if everything in the exhibition sold; during the run of the show, a newspaper strike all but eliminated reviews.

The rigorous beauty of Kurtz's work, halfway between the optical stringency of Stanczak and the lushness of

Figure 81. Jochen Seidel, *Train Your Mind*, 1963–67 (cat. no. 116)

J. M. W. Turner, is amply evident in her *Untitled (white)* (fig. 82). The shimmering color effects suggest a landscape of huge proportions, a gesture toward the aesthetic of the sublime in terms that are thoroughly modern and somewhat mystical. The vast spaces of skyscapes—sunrises and twilights, and even the starflecked depth of midnight—are recalled without being specifically pictured. This nonobjective art which makes no apparent gesture to nature, nevertheless, addresses that same grandness of nature as Richardson's sculpture. Kurtz was nearly the last artist to appear under the impress of the gallery while it was yet a public space; accordingly, her work is the most recent in the Martha Jackson Memorial Collection.

In time Anderson's artistic commitment was recognized, although his realtor's sense was not as strong as his aesthetics. SoHo continued to dominate the artistic scene and transform Manhattan's cultural, social, gastronomic, and gallery-going patterns. On the far western edge of 57th Street, the Martha Jackson Gallery was an enclave amidst an odd mixture of heavy industry, the world's perfume center, and the CBS television news headquarters. Few of the passersby guessed that by entering an unlikely looking building they would be admitted to a realm of sensation unlike anything in that part of the city. Yet, occasionally a spectator would recall that moment when artists' careers were marked by a slower, more deliberate trajectory, when dealers played a more relaxed and personal role intervening between the customer's delighted wonder and the artist's yearning for recognition and sales. Such an era, however far in spirit from our own, is only a generation past. Recollecting for readers of the *New York Times*, Peter Schjeldahl wrote:

> There were no price reports from the latest auction to establish what was important and what wasn't. That was a matter to be decided by individuals, each moved by his personal tastes and private passions.
>
> Prior to about 1960, American art dealers and collectors were relatively marginal celebrities; the best of them was characterized by dedication and sensitivity. Then art went big time, and new star-caliber dealers and collectors began to augment, if not replace, those old-fashioned qualities with such others as entrepreneurial shrewdness and daring. The "art world" was born.
>
> For people like the late Martha Jackson, one of the most prominent dealers of the day, the fashion-obsessed new art world was a distressing phenomena.[138]

Although the Martha Jackson Gallery became the David Anderson Gallery in time, eventually a deeper transformation made the gallery a merchants' gallery selling essentially to other dealers. The public no longer roamed the gallery discovering the new or rediscovering masterful personalities passed over in casual histories. For David Anderson, life altered dramatically without the day-to-day care of artists' careers to nurture, the press to allure and fend off, collectors to entice, cultivate, and inform, and the gallery stock to balance for all levels of the public budget. In a quiescent form the gallery still exists, not as a "shadow of its former self," but as a very different institution with different goals. He reflected upon the change in a letter to a friend:

> ...our decision in many respects mirrors another made by Martha in 1949 when she decided to quit her life as a homemaker in Buffalo and move to New York. When she left Buffalo she had as her purpose only to get away from the routines of that kind of life; she wanted to be a wife and homemaker no longer. Eventually, this new life of hers became my life as well; it has been grand and wonderful, but now I must travel that same road in the opposite direction, to provide a simpler, more rational lifestyle and stable secure future for my family.[139]

Figure 82. Elaine Kurtz, *Untitled (white)*, 1980 (cat. no. 95)

NOTES

1. Adelyn Breeskin, Preface in *The Private Collection of Martha Jackson* (College Park, Maryland: University of Maryland Art Gallery, 1973), 3. Although all recollections of Martha Jackson's introduction to the world of commercial art include similar anecdotes, with slight variations about which artist was her first purchase, it is difficult to locate the Museum of Modern Art exhibition that corresponds to these remembrances. The most likely Chagall exhibition was held at the museum (in collaboration with the Art Institute of Chicago) in 1946, the catalogue does not include a work borrowed from Martha Jackson or one that fits that distinctive description of her first purchase.

2. Ibid., 5.

3. Press release from the files of the David Anderson Gallery.

4. Seymour H. Knox, Foreword in *The Martha Jackson Collection at the Albright-Knox Gallery* (Buffalo, New York: Albright-Knox Gallery, 1975), 4.

5. Quoted in Nancy Tobin Willig, "Mrs. Jackson's Collection Right at Home at Albright," *Buffalo Courier-Express*, 27 January 1974, 4.

6. Eldzier Cortor, letter to the author, 25 July 1984.

7. "Cortor's Latest," *Washington Star*, 14 February 1954.

8. "Eldzier Cortor Work on View at Whyte's," *Washington Post*, 14 February 1954, Gallery Notes section.

9. Eldzier Cortor, letter to the author, 25 July 1984.

10. Harold Rosenberg, *Art on the Edge: Creators and Situations* (New York: MacMillan & Co., 1971), 231.

11. Sam Hunter, *James Brooks* (New York: Whitney Museum of American Art, 1963), 5.

12. Irving Sandler, *The Triumph of American Painting* (New York: Praeger Publishers, 1970), 233.

13. In a letter to the author, 4 June 1981, Brooks noted that he was gratified "with the information that your collection [the NMAA] now contains *Oran* and *Harmagh*, for I could not be represented by work that would please me more."

14. Joseph Masheck, Reviews, *Artforum* 12 (December 1973): 79.

15. James Brooks, in correspondence with the author, 24 August 1981.

16. Lillian Kiesler, in correspondence with the author, 8 August 1982.

17. Amy Baker Sandback, in correspondence with the author, 2 September 1982.

18. Kermit I. Lansner, Reviews and Previews, *Art News* 52 (February 1954): 42.

19. Ethel Schwabacher, Introduction, in *Gallery Urban Exhibition* (New York, 4 to 30 January 1954), n.p.

20. Meyer Schapiro, Introduction, *Gandy Brody* (Gray Gallery, Chicago, January 1967, and the Zabriskie Gallery, New York, March 1967), n.p.

21. Isaak Witkin, statement made at Gandy Brody's memorial service held at the New School for Social Research on 10 November 1975 and reprinted in the pamphlet that accompanied the exhibition, *Gandy Brody* (Knoedler and Co., 15 October to 4 November 1980), n.p.

22. Lawrence Calcagno, in correspondence with the author, December 1981.

23. Ibid.

24. Ibid.

25. Lawrence Campbell, "Lawrence Calcagno," *Art News* 54 (October 1955): 48.

26. Bryan Robertson writing in the catalogue of the exhibition, *Lawrence Calcagno* (McRoberts & Tunnard Gallery, London, 1961), stoutly supported the artist:

These paintings are landscapes of the mind, evocative of something past and invocations of something to come....They are full of a cosmic sense of the universe, and yet they are full of very explicit and subtly registered detail....The metaphysical implications of Calcagno's painting typify American art as a whole today: for a nation founded on an idea and not on blood must continually find itself through a series of abstractions. (p. 7).

27. Lawrence Calcagno, in correspondence with the author, December 1981.

28. Otis Gage, *Arts and Architecture* 72, no. 5 (May 1955): 10.

29. Robert Rosenblum, "John Hultberg," *Art Digest* 29 (15 April 1955): 22.

30. Lawrence Campbell, "John Hultberg," *Art News* 55 (March 1956): 51.

31. John Ashberry, "John Hultberg," *Art News* 56 (January 1958): 17.

32. James R. Mellow, "John Hultberg," *Arts Magazine* 34 (November 1959): 53. Other reviewers subsequently noted a similar sensation when viewing his work:

These recent paintings have a mood of peace, the peace that follows a railroad accident or that precedes the countdown before the pressing of a fatal button. (Lawrence Campbell, "John Hultberg," *Art News* 59 [February 1961]: 14.)

33. Lawrence Campbell, "John Hultberg," *Art News* 63 (December 1964): 15.

34. Kim Levin, "John Hultberg," *Art News* 69, no. 3 (May 1970): 67. Another reviewer carried this position even further, stating that "His vision is post-Futurist; a romantic recollection of ruins not yet created." (Joseph Dreiss, "John Hultberg," *Arts Magazine* 48, no. 7 [April 1974]: 64.)

35. Parker Tyler, Reviews and Previews, *Art News* 54 (February 1956): 51.

36. Sam Feinstein, A Gallery Itinerary, *Art Digest* 28 (April 1954): 21.

37. Benjamin Forgey, "An Art Show in Two Parts," *Washington Star*, 27 June 1973.

38. A.N., "International Group," *Art Digest* 28 (June 1954): 17.

39. Parker Tyler, Announcements, *Art News* 54 (May 1955): 51.

40. S. D. Edwards, letter to the author, April 1983.

41. When *Harper's Bazaar* chose "100 American Women of Accomplishment" in October 1967, among the handful of artistic personalities—painters, sculptors, and dealers—Martha Jackson was noted for "the strength of her personality, her objectivity and trenchant judgment [that] have served as a springboard for launching numerous artists in the gallery bearing her name."

42. Andrea O. Cohen, "The Power of Her Intuition," *Washington Post*, 22 June 1973, sec. B, p. 15.

43. Richard Diebenkorn, letter to the author, 1 June 1981.

44. Martha Jackson, "More in Art," *Mademoiselle* (1964).

45. Rosalind Constable, "Martha Jackson: An Appreciation," *Arts Magazine* 44 (September-October 1969): 18.

46. Julian Stanczak, letter to the author, 1 June 1981.

47. Joseph Mascheck, Reviews, *Artforum* 12 (December 1973): 73. The reviewer for *Connoisseur* (February 1974, 153) stated simply that "Eclectic in taste, each piece from Martha Jackson's collection is of the highest quality."

48. "Gilbert Sorrentino—An Interview," *Vort*, no. 6 (Fall 1974): 23.

49. Frank O'Hara, "Why I Am Not a Painter," *Collected Poems of Frank O'Hara*, ed. Donald Allen (New York: Alfred A. Knopf, Inc.). Copyright 1958 by Maureen Granville-Smith, administrix of the estate of Frank O'Hara. Reprinted by permission of Alfred A. Knopf, Inc. The poem is dated 1956 and was first published in *Evergreen Review* 1, no. 3 (1957); it was reprinted in the catalogue of the March-April 1966 exhibition of Michael Goldberg's work at the Martha Jackson Gallery.

50. James Schuyler, "Michael Goldberg," *Art News* 59, no. 1 (March 1960): 40.

51. George Dennison, "Michael Goldberg," *Arts Magazine* 33, no. 7 (1959): 60.

52. Irving Sandler, "Michael Goldberg," *Art News* 59, no. 7 (November 1960): 13. Jill Johnson saw in his technique for these pictures a style that "coordinates in some remote jigsaw fashion with the angularities of the loose exterior" (*Art News* 62, no. 9 [January 1964]: 12).

53. Norman Bluhm, "Art: Rice and Hamburger," *Newsweek* (28 April 1969): 91.

54. Thomas B. Hess, *Vernissage de l'Exposition: Norman Bluhm* (Galerie Anderson-Mayer, Paris, 28 April 1965). Another of Bluhm's Parisian exhibitions (Galerie Stadler, 21 May to 22 June 1968) consisted of ten works, two of which have been reunited in the NMAA's holdings: *Eudocia*, 1967 (1980.6.8), a gift of the Vincent Melzac Collection; *Mojabe*, 1966 (cat. no. 3), part of the Martha Jackson Memorial Collection.

55. Peter Schjeldahl, "A Dead Style? Bluhm Seems Not To Have Heard," *New York Times*, 3 May 1970, sec. II, p. 23, col. 1.

56. Another of the artists shown that season was Lee Krasner whose work was exhibited in February and March of 1958.

57. Michael Fried, *Morris Louis, 1912-1962* (Boston: Museum of Fine Arts, 1967) noted (p. 7) that "Greenberg has remarked that Louis might not have executed the series of paintings he later came to repudiate and destroy had he allowed himself to visit New York more often in order to see what kind of painting he did *not* want to do."

58. Frank Lobdell, in correspondence with the author, 10 July 1984. Lobdell continues:

Martha visited my studio for the last time in the winter of 1968. She was especially moved by a large yellow painting titled "Fall 1968" and asked me to send it to the gallery for an exhibition she planned for the summer of 1969. I gave the painting to the San Francisco Museum of Modern Art last year and titled it Fall 1968, in Memory of Martha Jackson.

59. Dore Ashton, "Este Gallery Show Spans 5 Centuries—Frank Lobdell's Work on View," *New York Times*, 19 April 1960, p. 34, col. 3.

60. George Dennison, In the Galleries, *Arts Magazine* 34 (May 1960): 56. This is a review of Lobdell's first solo exhibition in New York.

61. Irving Sandler, "Frank Lobdell," *Art News* 59 (May 1960): 19.

62. Donald Windham, "Fritz Bultman and New Orleans," *Fritz Bultman* (New Orleans: Isaac Delgado Museum of Art, 1959), n.p.

63. Irving Sandler, Reviews, *Art News* 57 (February 1959): 13.

64. Hilton Kramer remarked (*New York Times*, 24 January 1976, p. 22, col. 5) that, "These bronzes, while obviously the work of a serious artist, tend to rely on the familiar strategies of organic abstraction without adding much in the way of invention or surprise....They lack the intensity of a really personal iconography, which means they lack something essential."

65. April Kingsley, "Opening and Closing Fritz Bultman's Sculpture," *Arts Magazine* 50 (June 1976): 83.

66. Richard Lorber, "Fritz Bultman," *Arts Magazine* 50 (February 1976): 13.

67. Fritz Bultman, "Why I Draw From the Figure," *Drawings By Fritz Bultman* (New Orleans: New Orleans Museum of Art, March 1974), n.p. On another occasion, in a lighter mood, Bultman noted:

I draw for pleasure. My studio is a place of paint, canvas, water, plaster, and wire; it is for work, for reverie, for slow decisions, for changes that leave heaps of debris. I draw in my house, in my bedroom, and on porches where there are comfortable places for a model to recline, curves, elbows, hips cushioned. (Fritz

Bultman, "About My Drawings," *The Texas Quarterly* (Spring 1973): 71-passim.)

68. Fritz Bultman, "Portfolio: A Statement on Collage," *Cornell Review*, no. 6 (Summer 1979): 43.

69. Hilton Kramer, "Fritz Bultman Restates His Metaphors," *New York Times*, 24 January 1976, p. 22, col. 5.

70. Barbara Cavaliere, Reviews, *Arts Magazine* 51, no. 7 (March 1977): 28.

71. Douglas Crimp, "Reviews: Fritz Bultman," *Art News* 73 (March 1974): 99.

72. Quoted in Peter Selz, *Sam Francis* (New York: Harry N. Abrams, Inc., 1982), 20.

73. Hilton Kramer, "Francis: 'The Mallarmé of Painters'?" *New York Times*, 24 December 1972, sec. II, p. 25, col. 1. But Kramer continued:

The forms containing this color were devoid of inherent expressive interest...its essential emptiness derives from the very ease with which the artist took possession of his style in the earliest stages of his career. The struggle that other painters experience in transforming an inherently pictorial culture and wresting from it a personal statement of their own is nowhere apparent in Mr. Francis's work.

74. H. H. Arnason, *History of Modern Art* (New York: Harry N. Abrams, Inc., 1977), 679.

75. Hilton Kramer, "Sam Francis Focus of Whitney Display," *New York Times*, 16 December 1972, p. 27, col. 1. Kramer, for one found it

...fascinating that a young artist isolated from the dynamics of New York in the 1950s developed a pictorial style that resembles and parallels in so many ways what we have tended to think of as a New York style.

76. Louise Nevelson, letter to the author, 15 May 1981.

77. Dore Ashton, *American Art Since 1945* (New York: Oxford University Press, 1982), 59.

78. Martin Friedman, *Nevelson Wood Sculptures* (Minneapolis: Walker Art Center, 1973), 7.

79. Dore Ashton, "Art," *Art and Architecture* 76 (December 1959): 7.

80. Jack Kroll, Reviews and Previews, *Art News* 60 (May 1961): 10.

81. Jim Dine, letter to the author, 12 May 1981.

82. This aspect of his work was noted by David Shapiro, *Jim Dine: Painting What One Is* (New York: Harry N. Abrams, Inc., 1981), 19. He observed, "Some of Dine's earliest work immediately reminds us of the savagery and seriousness that has been part of his work despite its comical digressions."

83. Ibid., 20.

84. Rosalind Constable ("Martha Jackson: An Appreciation," *Arts Magazine* 44 [September-October 1969]: 18) continued her statement:

Martha did show Dine for a while, and she invited Kaprow to fill her backyard with old automobile tires, but she never really climbed on any of the new bandwagons. She stayed with her Abstract Expressionists even when interest in some of them waned. I wondered why, and one day I asked her. She looked at me in surprise, "I couldn't just desert all my artists," she said. And she never did.

85. John L. Goodyear, letter to the author, 25 July 1984.

86. Rosalind Constable, "Scouting Report on the Avant Garde," *Esquire* (June 1961): 88.

87. John Canaday, *New York Times*, Sunday 2 October 1960, sec. II, p. 21.

88. Ibid.

89. Peter Schjeldahl, "Before Art Went 'Big Time'," *New York Times*, 11 November 1973, sec. II, p. 21. Perhaps the period's most notable critic also felt a definite turning point was reached in the history of the gallery, but to Clement Greenberg this shift in the gallery's stance was not necessarily for the better. He wrote, "I esteemed Mrs. Jackson personally but admired what she did only up to a point." (Letter to the author, 28 July 1984.)

90. Joseph Mascheck, Reviews, *Artforum* 12 (December 1973): 80.

91. Michel Tapie, *Claire Falkenstein*, trans. Dorothy Cater (Rome: De Luca Art Monographs, 1958), 10.

92. A similar observation was made some years after *Conic's* date:

Much of Miss Falkenstein's metal sculpture is designed for an architectural environment. Without a suitable backdrop, the whole esthetic purpose of the work seems lost. (Jacqueline Barnitz, "Claire Falkenstein," *Arts Magazine* 39 [September 1965]: 72.)

93. Alex Katz, letter to the author, 15 July 1982.

94. Ibid.

95. Jill Johnston, Reviews and Previews, *Art News* 61 (Summer 1962): 47.

96. Irving Sandler and Bill Berkson, *Alex Katz* (New York: Praeger Publishers, 1971), vi.

97. Ibid., 27.

98. Irving Sandler, *New York Post,* 9 February 1964, In the Galleries section.

99. Irving Sandler, *The New York School: The Painters and Sculptors of the Fifties* (New York: Harper and Row, 1978), 115.

100. Grace Hartigan, letter to the author, 14 September 1981.

101. Ibid.

102. Lester Johnson, letter to the author, 2 October 1984.

103. Dore Ashton, "New York Commentary," *Studio* 165 (March 1963): 117.

104. Martha Jackson, letter to Jo and Lester Johnson, 30 June 1966.

105. Martha Jackson, letter to Lester Johnson, 24 February 1967.

106. Burt Chernow, *The Kaleidoscopic Crowd* (New York: David Anderson Gallery, 1975), 10.

107. John Ashberry, "Phillip Pavia," *Art News* 65 (January 1967): 17.

108. Meyer Schapiro, statement in exhibition catalogue for Wollman Hall, New School for Social Research, New York, 1969, n.p.

109. Peter Schjeldahl, "For Thompson, A Triumph Too Late," *New York Times,* 23 February 1969, sec. II, p. 31–32.

110. Julian Stanczak, letter to the author, 1 June 1981. Stanczak continued:

By the way, Josef Albers did come to see the show. He responded most favorably to the work, but never accepted the term. He wrote in a complimentary note to me, that the name for this kind of visual concern should be, "perceptual art."

111. Ibid.

112. Not all of the gallery's artists enjoyed unalloyed harmony in their business dealings. Lawrence Calcagno, ultimately Martha Jackson's admirer, remembers some of the legitimate disagreements that arose between them. He recalls (correspondence with the author, December 1981):

I sold paintings outside of New York, where I was teaching as visiting artist in universities. After one school year at the University of Alabama . . . I was invited to teach senior studio classes at the Albright School of the University of Buffalo. My situation was enhanced because of my connections with Martha, who was from a prominent family there. . . . I should have liked to have stayed in New York to paint instead of having to teach in the provinces for salaries as low as four thousand-two hundred dollars a year! I feel that had she been more generous and astute, she could easily have arranged this.

In the Autumn of 1959, after a year as visiting artist at the University of Illinois, I accepted part-time teaching at New York University, so that I could remain in New York City in closer association with Martha and her gallery. . . . In the Spring of that year she arranged a one-person exhibition of my work on paper at the Philadelphia Art Alliance. She accompanied me there for the opening and the dinner reception. We returned to New York City by train late in the evening. During the trip she questioned me about my work. She asserted that my paintings were very difficult to sell because they were so dark. I rebutted that serious work was always more difficult to sell than superficial work. She said that Sidney Janis, another successful dealer in New York, said that whatever sells is

good art. This angered me. She declared that dealers were valorous figures in the art world because they rescued artists from poverty and obscurity and enabled them to get on with their work. I retorted that if the walls of their galleries remained bare, dealers might have some difficulty finding their identities and purpose. For who exactly would Martha Jackson be if the five floors of her elegant building near Madison Avenue were barren of any works of art?

113. Emilio Cruz, in a letter to the author, June 1981.

114. Richard Lorber, Recent Acquisitions, *Arts Magazine* 50 (December 1975): 23.

115. Ian Ball, "Figures of State: Sculpture by Marisol," *The Daily Telegraph Magazine,* p. 20; "Marisol . . . A Brilliant Sculptress Shapes the Heads of State," *Look* (November 14, 1967): 78–83.

116. Ed McGowin, letter to the author, 21 July 1981.

In my work, I had established a direct link between Hans Hofmann's push and pull theory of abstract expressionism and the potential for transparancies and its ability to release color. In effect, to extend Hofmann's theory about surface tension, I had gone directly to painting on a non-surface or transparent surface. Martha was very keen about the connection to the rules of painting.

117. Ed McGowin, letter to the author, 21 May 1981. One piece sold from that show.

118. Author's correspondence with Stanley Dean Edwards.

119. Harold Rosenberg, *Art on the Edge* (New York: MacMillan & Co., 1971), 80-81.

120. James Harithas, Introduction in *"My Five Years in the Country:" Forty-Five Paintings by Joan Mitchell* (Syracuse: Everson Museum of Art, 1972), ii.

121. Ibid., iii.

122. Sandler, *The New York School,* 69.

123. Harold Rosenberg, *Art on the Edge,* 81.

124. Vivien Raynor, "7 Abstractions by Norman Bluhm on L.I.," *New York Times,* 13 July 1984, sec. C, p. 17.

125. Dennis Byng, letter to the author, 3 July 1984.

126. Ibid. Byng did get a chance to exercise his technical mastery on an unheard-of scale when, in 1973, he completed a commission for the State of New York's South Mall Legislative Building in Albany, a sixty-five foot cast lucite sculpture.

127. Michael Benedikt, "Dennis Byng," *Art News* 68 (October 1969): 13–14.

128. Jean-Louis Bourgeois, *Artforum* 8 (November 1969): 75.

129. Sam Richardson, letter to the author, 2 August 1984.

130. Carter Ratcliff, *Art International* 13 (December 1969): 72.

131. Natalie Edgar, "Sam Richardson," *Art News* 68 (November 1969): 86.

132. Ratcliff, *Art International* 13 (December 1969): 72.

133. Gerrit Henry, *Art International* 15 (January 1971): 42.

134. Peter Frank, "Jochen Seidel," *Art News* 74, no. 1 (January 1975): 112.

135. Peter Frank, "New Forms, New Media, New Space," *The Art Gallery Magazine* (March 1975): 15.

136. "New York Today: Some Artists Comments," *Art in America* 65, no. 5 (September 1977): 78–79.

137. Quoted in Elaine Kurtz, letter to the author, 3 November 1981.

138. Peter Schjeldahl, "Before Art Went 'Big Time'," *New York Times,* 11 November 1973, sec. II, p. 21, col. 7.

139. Quoted in Elaine Kurtz, letter to the author, 3 November 1981. The twelve-year commitment of a new lease on the gallery's building meant his growing family might have to endure his greatly diminished attentions as he ran the gallery, attentions that his mother divided between her gallery and family.

Exhibition History
of the
Martha Jackson Gallery

1953

24 March–28 April
100 Years of American Watercolors (Charles Burchfield, Arthur B. Davies, Arthur Dove, Philip Evergood, Lyonel Feininger, John Singer Sargent, Everett Shinn, James Abbott McNeil Whistler)

28 April–9 May
Lewis Kimball: Recent Oils and Watercolors

12–28 May
Selected Oils from the 1952 Carnegie International (Milton Avery, James Brooks, Willem de Kooning, Hans Hofmann, Ben Nicholson, Antoni Tapies)

2–26 June
Reginald March: Recent Drawings (The Jelke Trial and the Legendary Mizners)

Summer
Paintings from the Martha Jackson Gallery Collection (Max Beckmann, Marc Chagall, Willem de Kooning, Lyonel Feininger, Hans Hofmann, Georgia O'Keeffe, Mark Tobey, Stanton MacDonald-Wright, Philip Evergood, Arshile Gorky, Henry Moore, Ben Nicholson)

15 September–3 October
Women (Twenty-three artists, including Milton Avery, Max Beckmann, Willem de Kooning, Childe Hassem, Yasuo Kuniyoshi, Marie Laurencin, Henri Matisse, Jules Pascin, Pablo Picasso, Jean-Auguste Renoir, Larry Rivers)

8–24 October
William Getman: Oils and Collages from Mexico

28 October–14 November
Antoni Tapies

18 November–5 December
Seymour Drumlevitch: Paintings of Italy 1950-52

9–26 December
Carl Ruggles: A Composer Paints

10 December–9 January 1954
Potpourri of Pictures (eighteen works of young artists including Clay Bartlett, Charles Brady, Robert Cato, Eldzier Cortor, Frances Field, Gandy Brody, William Getman, Esther Goetz, Cecile Holzinger, Rebecca James, Edward Kaspar, Lewis Kimball, Alexander Luke, Antoni Tapies, Rudy Pozzatti, Allen Ullman)

1954

13–30 January
Clay Bartlett: Paintings of the West Indies

3–28 February
American Paintings from the Collection of Martha Jackson and Others

3–27 March
New Talent (including Alberto Burri, Lawrence Calcagno, Robert Cato, Paul Heller, Paul Haller Jones, Rudy Pozzatti)

8–24 March
Marion Humfeld: Scenes of India (at the Studio Club, 210 East 77th Street, New York City)

31 March–24 April
Arshile Gorky: Middle Period

Heinz Troekes: Recent Watercolors and Gouaches

18 May–12 June
Younger American and European Artists (Alberto Burri, Robert Cato, Lawrence Calcagno, Seymour Drumlevitch, Frances Field, William Getman, John Hultberg, Paul Haller Jones, Rudy Pozzatti, William Scott, Antoni Tapies, Heinz Troekes)

21 September–9 October
Rebecca Salisbury James: Paintings on Glass

21 October–9 November
British Artists: Hepworth-Bacon-Scott

8 November–4 December
Rudy Pozzatti

6–31 December
Karel Appel

1955

3–29 January
Marsden Hartley: The Berlin Period 1913-1915

31 January–26 February
German Painting Today (Willi Baumeister, Rolf Cavel, Hans Janisch, Heinz Troekes, Hans Ukman, Fritz Winter)

28 February–19 March
Robert Cato and Lawrence Kupperman: Experiments in New Techniques

21 March–9 April
Seymour Boardman

11–30 April
John Hultberg

2–14 May
Grace Borgenicht

16 May–11 June
Eight New Decade Painters (Karel Appel, Francis Bacon, Maria Helena Vieira da Silva, Willem de Kooning, Jean Dubuffet, Franz Kline, William Scott)

13–30 June
Paul Haller Jones

27 September–15 October
Lawrence Calcagno

17 October–5 November
Marino Marini (gouaches and drawings)

9 November–3 December
Willem de Kooning (oils and drawings, 1954-55)

5–23 December
Matthew Barnes: 1880-1951

EXHIBITIONS AT 32 EAST 69TH STREET

1956

24 January–11 February
Opening Exhibition of New Martha Jackson Gallery: Paintings and Sculpture from the Collection of Martha Jackson (including Fritz Winter, Arshile Gorky, Adolph Gottlieb, Willem de Kooning, Paul Haller Jones, Seymour Drumlevitch, Hans Hofmann, Lyonel Feininger, Max Beckmann, John Marin, Francis Bacon, Jean Dubuffet, Ben Nicholson, William Scott, Paul Borduas, Franz Kline, Jackson Pollock, Karel Appel, Seymour Boardman, John Hultberg, Paul Jenkins, Alberto Burri, Robert Cato, Antoni Tapies, Barbara Hepworth, Henry Moore)

13 February–3 March
Sam Francis

6–31 March
John Hultberg: Recent Paintings
Louise Kruger: Sculpture

30 March–7 April
Paul Jenkins

3–21 April
Seymour Boardman: Recent Paintings

5–29 June
Outdoor Sculpture Exhibition (fourteen American sculptors, including Ibram Lassaw, Peter Grippe, Jose de Creeft, Nat Werner, Doris Caesar, Jeanne Reynal, Constantino Nivola, Phy Caparn [Mrs. Johannes Steel], Fred Farr, Richard Stankiewicz, [Barnett?] Newman, Albert T. Terris, Guitou Knoop)

1–17 October
Salute to Modern Art USA

2–27 October
William Getman: Collages from Old Mexico

1955–56
Barbara Hepworth: Carving and Drawings, 1937-54 (traveled throughout the United States and Canada)

29 October–17 November
William Scott: Paintings and Drawings

13 November–1 December
Sophy Regensburg

26 November–15 December
Harry Jackson: Paintings and Drawings

1–31 December
Art for Christmas (small-scale works by Karel Appel, Alberto Burri, Marc Chagall, Adolph Gottlieb, Marsden Hartley, Barbara Hepworth, John Hultberg, Paul Klee, Marino Marini, Henry Moore, Pablo Picasso, Germaine Richier, William Scott)

1957

19–26 January
Barbara Hepworth: Sculpture, Paintings, Drawings

29 January–23 February
Adolph Gottlieb (twenty oils, 1952–56)

21 February–14 March
Antoni Tapies: Recent Paintings

18 March–6 April
Paul-Emile Borduas: Paintings 1953–56

9 April–11 May
New Aspects of Space (twenty works, including pieces by Karel Appel, Norman Bluhm, Seymour Boardman, Lawrence Calcagno, Sam Francis, John Hultberg, Alfred Leslie)

8 May–15 June
Drawings in Color and Black and White

19 May–14 June
Marsden Hartley: Landscapes and Still-lives

1–26 October
Karel Appel

29 October–23 November
Sculpture for Museum Collections (fourteen works, 1936–56)

5–23 November
Morris Louis (eleven oils)

27 November–27 December
Sam Francis (sixteen watercolors, 1954–57)
Germaine Richier: Sculpture (twenty-seven bronzes, 1944–57)

1958

2–25 January
John Hultberg: Recent Paintings (1956–57)

28 January–22 February
Lawrence Calcagno (ten oils, 1957; six watercolors and gouaches, 1956–57)
Louise Kruger (twenty sculptures)

24 February–22 March
Lee Krasner

1–26 April
Norman Carton: Recent Paintings (fourteen abstract oils)

29 April–29 May
Harold Altman (drawings)

1–30 June
Ten Block Exhibition (Madison Avenue between 64th and 74th Streets)

25 September–25 October
The Gutai Group

28 October–22 November
Paul Jenkins (twenty large paintings)

25 November–20 December
Sam Francis (eleven canvases, two watercolors)

1959

2–23 January
The Enormous Room: Four Artists (four mural-size works by Alfred Leslie, Fritz Bultman, Sam Francis, Michael Goldberg; John Chamberlain, *Gate*, iron and steel sculpture, situated outside room)
Hisao Domoto

27 January–21 February
Fritz Bultman (paintings, 1957; twenty-six oils; seven drawings)

24 February–21 March
Antoni Tapies (sixteen works)

24 March–18 April
William Scott (recent paintings)
Norman Carton (eleven paintings)
Paul-Emile Borduas (black and white paintings)

22 April–18 May
Sofu Teshigahara
Alfred Jensen

19 May–19 June
Walasse Ting
The New York Scene (from *Enormous Room*; fifteen oil, one sculpture, one ink drawing)

10 September–3 October
Karel Appel, Rudy Pozzatti, Germaine Richier

6–24 October
John Hultberg: New Paintings Matisse to Manessier (selected twentieth-century paintings)

29 October–21 November
Louise Nevelson: Sky Columns Presence

10 November–1 December
Picasso: Graphics (nine lithographs; six dry-point etchings, 1944; six unique ceramics)

24 November–19 December
Alfred Jensen

10 December–2 January
Prints and Paintings

1960

5–30 January
Alfred Leslie: Paintings
John Chamberlain: Sculptures (from *Enormous Room*)

2–27 February
Alberto Burri (works, 1955–59)

27 February–19 March
Gottfried Honegger (15 paintings, 1959–60)

1–19 March
Michael Goldberg

22 March–16 April
Lawrence Calcagno
Antoni Tapies (lithographs)

19 April–7 May
Frank Lobdell: 1953–59

23 April–2 May
Walasse Ting

6–24 June
New Forms—New Media I (including Stephen Antonakos, Lee Bontecou, Alberto Burri, Chryssa, Joseph Cornell, Jim Dine)

8–24 September
Four Japanese Artists

28 September–22 October
New Forms—New Media II (including Robert Indiana, Jasper Johns, Louise Nevelson, Robert Rauschenberg, John Chamberlain, Dan Flavin, Claes Oldenburg, Henry Moore)

25 October–19 November
Karel Appel: Paintings 1955–60 (gouaches)

22 November–17 December
Michael Goldberg: Recent Paintings (fourteen paintings)

20 December–14 January
The Internationals (Francis Bacon, Paul-Emile Borduas, Alberto Burri, Enrico Donati, Michael Goldberg, Gottfried Honegger, Philippe Hosiasson, John Hultberg, Paul Jenkins, Alfred Jensen, Franz Kline, Frank Lobdell, Georges Mathieu, Larry Rivers, William Scott, Antoni Tapies)

1961

18 January–14 February
Alfred Jensen

20 January–18 February
Larry Rivers (seven sculptures 1959–60; lithographs at David Anderson Gallery)

14 February–11 March
John Hultberg: New Paintings (fifteen oils, three gouaches)

15 March–8 April
Antoni Tapies

20 April–20 May
Louise Nevelson: The Royal Tides (gold sculpture, black-and-white walls)
Marsden Hartley (paintings and drawings at the David Anderson Gallery)

25 May–23 June
Environments, Situations, Spaces (George Brecht, Jim Dine, Walter Gaudnek, Allan Kaprow, Claes Oldenburg, Robert Whitman, at David Anderson Gallery)

3–21 October
Paul Jenkins: Recent Painting

24 October–18 November
Alan Davie (at David Anderson Gallery)

21 November–16 December
Lucio Fontana (with David Anderson Gallery)

11 December–6 January
Motonaga

1962

9 January–3 February
Jim Dine (with David Anderson Gallery)

24 January–17 February
Louise Nevelson

3 February–1 March
Arshile Gorky: Drawings 1929–34

6 February–3 March
Selections 1934–1961 of American Artists from the Collection of Martha Jackson

6–31 March
Alfred Leslie: Paintings (ten oils, 1961–62)

3–26 April
Lawrence Calcagno (drawings, 1961–62)

28 April–26 May
John Hultberg (at David Anderson Gallery)

1–26 May
Billy Al Bengston (fourteen works, 1961–62)

5–30 June
Alex Katz: Stage Sets for "George Washington Crossing the Delaware"

25 September–20 October
William Scott: Paintings in Retrospect 1952–62

23 October–17 November
Grace Hartigan (eight oils)

20 November–15 December
Philippe Hosiasson

23 November–29 December
Sculpture International (Yaacov Agam, Karel Appel, Hans Arp, John Chamberlain, Dušan Džamonja, Sorel Etrog, Claire Falkenstein, Lucio Fontana, Jacques Lipchitz, Marino Marini, Louise Nevelson, Arnaldo Paolozzi)

18 December–5 January
Painting International (including Alfred Jensen, Larry Rivers, Antoni Tapies, Alan Davie, Asger Jorn, Alfred Leslie, Morris Louis, John Hultberg, Alberto Burri, Julius Bissier, Sam Francis)

1963

8 January–2 February
Lester Johnson
Michael Goldberg (ten oils)

5 February–2 March
Jean McEwen: Paintings (fifteen oils, two ink drawings, 1961–62)

15 February–5 March
Recent Prints and Paintings (at Premier Gallery, Minneapolis)

5–30 March
Karel Appel: Paintings, Sculpture, Graphic Works, Books

2–27 April
John Hultberg (paintings, 1962; nineteen lithographs)

30 April–21 May
Frank Lobdell: Paintings and Drawings (ten paintings)

23–29 May
Artists for CORE (benefit sale for the Congress of Racial Equality)

May–June
Louise Nevelson Bronzes and Other Sculpture (six bronze gates; works by other gallery artists)

4–22 June
Galerie Pilotes, Lausanne (selections from the Martha Jackson Gallery)

17 September–12 October
Eleven Americans

15 October–16 November
Antoni Tapies

9–30 November
Yves Gaucher

19 November–16 December
Christo Capralos

3 December–4 January
Bob Thompson

1964

7 January–1 February
Michael Goldberg: Still Lifes Group Exhibition (including Mark Tobey, Karel Appel, Antoni Tapies, Arshile Gorky)

4-29 February
Lester Johnson: Bowery Series (selected drawings, 1958-63)

3-28 March
Paul Jenkins: Recent Paintings 1963-64

31 March-25 April
Karel Appel: Object Paintings

28 April-25 May
Sam Francis: New Lithographs

1-31 May
Sculpture

26 May-14 August
Looking Back: A Survey of Gallery Exhibitions

8-26 September
Julian Stanczak (eighteen works)

18-26 September
New Acquisitions (twenty works, including Fernand Leger, Alexander Calder, Joseph Cornell, Arshile Gorky, Paul Klee, Jean Dubuffet, Amadeo Modigliani, Viktor Vasarely)

29 September-17 October
Jay Milder: Subway Runaway Series (twenty paintings)

17 October-19 November
Gottfried Honegger: Paintings in Relief (thirty-one works)

20 October-21 November
John Hultberg: White Paintings (fourteen paintings, a retrospective 1952-60)

24 November-19 December
Grace Hartigan: New Paintings 1963-64 (fourteen paintings)

15-30 December
Christmas Exhibition: Watercolors and Gouaches from the Private Collection of Mrs. Winchester Fitch Ingersoll (more than fifty works)
Christmas Exhibition of Gallery Artists (Bob Thompson, John Hultberg, Karel Appel, Lester Johnson, Grace Hartigan, Wendy Vanderbilt, Paul Jenkins)

1965

6-31 January
Vibrations Eleven: The Anomina Group and Others

9 February-6 March
Figuration (thirty-six works)

9 March-3 April
Alan Davie (twenty-two works, 1963-64)

6 April-1 May
International 4: Collages and Constructions (forty works)

4 May-18 June
Claire Falkenstein: Sculpture and Kinetic Paintings 1963-64 (sixty works)

21 September-9 October
Group Exhibition (Hans Hofmann, Paul Jenkins, Antoni Tapies, Yves Gaucher, Adolph Gottlieb, Ronald Pearson, Claire Falkenstein, Michael Goldberg)
Bob Thompson: New Paintings 1964-65

12-30 October
Julian Stanczak: New Paintings 1965

2-27 November
Alik Cavaliere (bronze sculptures)

5 November
Sale of original works and graphics

30 November-30 December
Selections for Museums Acquisition: Paintings and Sculpture

1966

4-29 January
Carlos Merida: Recent Paintings 1962-65 (twenty-seven paintings)

8 March-April
Michael Goldberg: Recent Paintings 1964-65 (twenty paintings)

6-30 April
Edward Weiss: Portraits of People of Renown (twenty-five paintings)

6 May-10 June
Frederick Kiesler: Sculpture 1964-65 (twenty-five pieces)

14 June-1 July
Phillip Pavia: Marble Sculpture (eleven pieces)

13 September-1 October
Yves Gaucher: Recent Paintings 1965-66

4–29 October
**John Hultberg: Paintings and Lithographs
1965–66** (twenty-four works)

11–26 November
Paul Jenkins: Paintings 1965–66 (twenty-two paintings)

26 November–30 December
Small Sculptures and Sculptors Drawings

29 November–30 December
Phillip Pavia: Marble Sculptures 1965–66
(twelve pieces)

1967

10 January–4 February
Karel Appel: Personnage Paintings 1965–66
(twenty-five paintings)

7 February–4 March
Grace Hartigan: Oils 1966 (twelve paintings)

7 March–1 April
Hisao Domoto: Solutions de Continuite 1966–67
(nineteen paintings)

March 1967–May 1968
Martha Jackson Traveling Exhibition (including
four works each by Lester Johnson, John Hultberg, Grace
Hartigan, Michael Goldberg, Karel Appel, Paul Jenkins)

4–29 April
Antoni Tapies: Mixed Media 1965–66
(fifteen paintings)

2–27 May
Frank Roth: Recent Painting 1966

3–23 June
Young Artists

26 September–7 October
Celine Chalem: Tables You Can Eat On
(ten sculptures)

17 October–18 November
Treasures from Inventory I: Seventeen Loves
(Fifteenth Anniversary Celebration, 1953–68)

21 November–23 December
A Christmas Show: Treasures from Inventory II
(fifty works)

30 December–13 January
Treasures from Inventory III
**Jim Dine: Paintings, Drawings, and Collages
1958–61** (nineteen works)

1968

16–31 January
Alfred Jensen: Paintings 1958–60 (fourteen paintings)

2 February–3 March
James Brooks: Recent Paintings 1966–67
(fourteen paintings)

5–28 March
**Bob Thompson: Important Works in New York
Collections** (twenty-five paintings)

2–27 April
Joan Mitchell (seventeen paintings)

30 March–20 April
Man Ray: Multiple Sculpture (fourteen works
from Europe)

27 April–18 May
Paul Jenkins: Watercolors

30 April–23 May
Frank Roth: Paintings and Sculpture

20 May–22 June
Gallery Group Show (including Karel Appel, Enrico
Donati, John Hultberg, Grace Hartigan, Lester Johnson, Paul
Jenkins, Joan Mitchell, Antoni Tapies, Gio Pomodoro, Claire
Falkenstein)

28 May–22 June
**Ed McGowin: Plastic Sculptures and Sculpture
Drawings**

17 September–5 October
Clayton Pond

8–30 October
New Acquisitions (including Francis Bacon, Aristide
Maillol, Lynn Chadwick, Gio Pomodoro, Harry Bertoia, Jean-
Paul Riopelle, Paul Klee, Henry Moore, Willem de Kooning,
Barbara Hepworth, Masayuki Nagare, Ossip Zadkine)
Hans Hofmann: Oils and Inks on Paper
(thirty-one works)

1–30 November
**Antoni Tapies: Recent Paintings and Works on
Paper 1966–67**

3–28 December
Julian Stanczak: Paintings 1968
Canadian Graphics Show

16–31 December
Selections from the Graphics Department

1968–69

Lester Johnson: The New Vein and the Human Figure 1963–68 (tour throughout Europe and South America arranged through the Smithsonian)

1969

4–25 January

John Hultberg: Recent Paintings 1968
(thirteen paintings)

Sculpture/Prints/Drawings by Sculptors (including Lucio Fontana, Ed McGowin, Henry Moore, Louise Nevelson, Eduardo Paolozzi, Alexander Calder, Lynn Chadwick, Sorel Etrog, Claire Falkenstein)

1–22 February

Lester Johnson: Figures 1968 (eighteen paintings)
Frank Roth: Drawings and Collages 1968–69

1–22 March

Paul Jenkins: Recent Paintings 1968–69

29 March–19 April

Aijiro Wakita: White Wound Sculpture (Garo Zareh)

Antreasian: The Silver Suite (nineteen lithographs in silver foil)

26 April–28 May

Phillip Pavia: Marble Sculptures 1967–68
(fifteen pieces)

Nathan Oliveira: Lithographs

4–20 June

Wallworks Part I

24 June–18 July

Wallworks Part II

31 July–31 August

Paintings (at the John Bolles Gallery, San Francisco)

9–27 September

Dennis Byng: Plexiglass Constructions
(eighteen pieces)

14 September–14 October

From the Martha Jackson Gallery (Martha Jackson Memorial at the Esther Bear Gallery, Santa Barbara, California)

4–25 October

Sam Richardson: Sculpture Landscapes
(thirty pieces)

1–22 November

Karel Appel: Paintings and Sculpture
(twenty-four pieces)

3–20 December

Louise Nevelson: Black Walls and Sculptures
(twenty works, 1950s)

1970

3–24 January

Lucio Fontana: Twelve Paintings 1960–62
Gio Pomodoro: Graphics

27–31 January

An Exhibition and Sale for the Studio Museum in Harlem

3–21 February

Frank Roth: Recent Paintings 1969–70

28 February–21 March

Paul Jenkins: Recent Paintings 1969–70
(twenty paintings)

28 March–18 April

Grace Hartigan: Oils and Collages 1969–70
(eighteen works)

22 April–9 May

Norman Bluhm: Recent Paintings 1968–69
(sixteen paintings)

15–30 May

John Hultberg: Paintings 1969 (nine paintings)
Gordon Smith: Serigraphs 1968–69

2–26 June

Wallworks III
Wallworks III Graphics

15 September–3 October

Martha Jackson Graphics (Second Annual)

6–31 October

Antoni Tapies: Paintings and Drawings from the Gallery Collection 1969–70

13–31 October

Sorel Etrog: Graphics and Books

3–28 November

Sam Francis: Paintings, Watercolors and Gouaches 1950–69

Sam Richardson: Islands and Ice/Sculpture 1970
(eleven pieces)

4–19 December

December Group Show (including Clayton Pond, Grace Hartigan, James Brooks, Paul Jenkins, Joan Mitchell, Karel Appel, Frank Roth, Norman Bluhm, Enrico Donati, Julian Stanczak)

Aijiro Wakita: Sculpture and Graphics
(twelve pieces)

1971

5–30 January
Julian Stanczak: Recent Paintings 1969–70
(thirty paintings)
Norman Bluhm: Triptychs (fourteen paintings)

3–27 February
James Brooks: Recent Paintings (1969–70)

2–27 March
Lester Johnson: The Human Situation (thirty
paintings, 1970)
Julian Stanczak: Serigraphs (1970; published by
Martha Jackson with Denise Rene Gallery)

30 March–24 April
Hisao Domoto: Solutions de Continuites
(twenty-seven paintings)
Karel Appel (1970 lithographs; published by
Martha Jackson)

8 May–2 June
Gio Pomodoro: Contatti (seven sculptures, 1970)

16 June–16 July
Karel Appel: Chelsea People (nineteen oils, 1970)
**David Gilhooly: Antedeluvian Frogs and Other
Primitive Ancestors** (ceramic sculptures, 1970–71)

7–25 September
Third Annual Graphics Exhibition
Exhibition at the Seibu Department Store (Tokyo)

29 September–16 October
Frank Roth: Recent Acrylics (thirteen canvases)
Jesus Raphael Soto: Eight Kinetic Reliefs (1964–66)

20 October–13 November
Karel Appel: Reliefs, Sculpture and Paintings
Sam Francis: Sunlight and Shadows (lithographs)

17 November–18 December
Paul Jenkins: Phenomena Ore Lode Vein
Bruce Lowney (lithographs)

1972

4–29 January
**Concept and Content: John Cage, Antoni Tapies,
Bob Thompson**

2–26 February
Eric H. Olson: Optochromic Objects (sixteen works)
John Hultberg: Landscape in Retrospect
(twenty-three paintings, 1954–71)

1–25 March
Frank Lobdell: Paintings 1968–71 (twenty-two paint-
ings and gouaches)
From the "Fifties" (works on paper, including Alexander
Calder, Mark Tobey, Sam Francis, Philip Guston, Franz
Kline, Willem de Kooning, Alfred Leslie, Lester Johnson,
James Brooks, Hans Hofmann)

28 March–22 April
Norman Bluhm: Recent Painting (thirteen paintings,
1970–71)
Julian Stanczak: Progressions 1971

26 April–13 May
Joan Mitchell: Blue Series (Part One, 1970–71)

16 May–26 June
Joan Mitchell: The Field Series (Part Two, 1971–72)
Clayton Pond: Parts of Things (twelve acrylics,
1970–71)

3–28 October
**Sam Richardson: Landscape Sculpture,
Embossed Drawings, Dimensional Studies**

4–25 November
Mark Tobey: Graphics

8–28 November
James Brooks: Recent Paintings (Part One)

29 November–31 December
James Brooks: Paintings 1949–72 (Part Two)
Richard Diebenkorn: Lithographs

1973

3 January–20 February
Faces

5 January–16 February
William Scott: Paintings 1970–72

28 February–24 March
Lester Johnson: Paintings 1971–73

22 February–17 March
Antoni Tapies: Works on Paper

27 March–21 April
Paul Jenkins: Watercolors

21 April–19 May
Fritz Bultman: Small Sculpture and Collages

24 April–19 May
Julian Stanczak: Recent Paintings

5–22 June
New Images (in collaboration with fourteen "Uptown" Galleries' *New Talent Festival*)

12 September–6 October
Karel Appel: The Early Fifties 1950–56 (thirty-five works of painting, gouache, drawing from the COBRA period)

10 October–3 November
Alma W. Thomas: Paintings

7 November–15 December
Antoni Tapies 1969–72 (twenty-four works)

8 November–1 December
Antoni Tapies: Graphics

2–21 December
Holiday Group Graphics Show

1974

5–26 January
Fritz Bultman Collages: Bridges Between Sculpture and Painting
Elaine Breiger: Graphics

31 January–20 February
John Hultberg: Paintings 1972–73
Group Exhibition (Julian Stanczak, Alma Thomas, James Brooks, Joan Mitchell, Lester Johnson, Norman Bluhm, Clayton Pond)

20 January–22 February
Mark Tobey: Graphics

23 February–17 March
Keith Boyle: Collages

26 February–23 March
Tom Parish: Paintings

20 March–6 April
Sam Richardson: Graphics (published by Martha Jackson)

27 March–20 April
Francisco Toledo

10–27 April
Sam Francis: New Graphics

30 April–12 May
Lester Johnson: Graphics and Works on Paper

23 April–18 May
Norman Bluhm

24 May–14 June
Dennis Byng: Cast Lucite Sculptures
Aijiro Wakita: Sculpture
Peter Spinelli: Cement Works

19 September–12 October
Herb Aach: Precession of the Equinoxes

5–26 October
David Hayes: Ceramics

17 October–16 November
Frank Lobdell: Paintings and Drawings 1955–73

29 October–16 November
New Acquisitions: Graphics

20 November–18 December
Jochen Seidel: Paintings

23 November–18 December
Antoni Tapies: Poems from the Catalan (with Joan Brossa)

1975

3 January–1 February
William Scott: Drawings

1–27 February
Clayton Pond: Capital Ideas (serigraphs published by Martha Jackson)

5 February–1 March
Sam Richardson: Sierra Snow Series 1973–74 (with corresponding exhibition at the Hanson-Fuller Gallery, San Francisco)

1–27 March
Bob Thompson: Drawings

6–29 March
Lester Johnson: City Women

29 March–1 May
Black and White (selected etchings and lithographs from the gallery's collection)

1–26 April
Julian Stanczak: Recent Paintings
Benefit for the Once Gallery at Martha Jackson West (special video by Nam June Paik and video cello by Charlotte Moorman)

8–26 April
Inaugural Exhibition Part One (Martha Jackson West, including conceptual artists Billy Apple, Stefan Eims, Dietor Froese, Jane Greer, Philippa Quarrell)

30 April–24 May
James Brooks: Recent Paintings 1973–75

3–24 May
Francisco Toledo: Recent Etchings and Aquatints

6–24 May
Inaugural Exhibition Part Two (Martha Jackson West, including conceptual artists Jacki Apple, Nancy Wilson Kitchell, Richard Quarrell, Martha Wilson)

31 May–20 June
Director's Choice: Five Printmakers

27 September–7 November
Acquisitions 1970–75

8 November–13 December
Antoni Tapies: Selected New Works 1973–74

1976
———————————————————

7 January–7 February
Bruce Lowney: New Lithographs

10 January–7 February
Fritz Bultman: Bronze Sculpture 1963–75

12 February–6 March
Graphics from the International Institute of Experimental Printmaking, Santa Cruz, California

13 March–3 April
Bob Thompson 1937–66: A Tribute (exhibition originated by the National Collection of Fine Arts [NMAA], Smithsonian Institution)
William Scott: Gouaches

7 April–1 May
Jochen Seidel: Word Drawings
Louis Comtois: Paintings

5 May–5 June
John Hultberg: Recent Paintings

5 May–2 July
James Brooks: Variations on a Theme (series of twelve lithographs)

9 June–2 July
Salute to '76 (works from gallery artists)

25 September–16 October
Group Exhibition (at 69th Street)
David Hockney Graphics: Six Fairy Tales from the Brothers Grimm

━━━━━━━━━━━━━━━━━━━━━━━━━━━━━━━━━━━━━

23 October–17 November
Sam Richardson
Alma Thomas: Recent Paintings 1975–76

20 November–18 December
Karel Appel: Paintings of the '60s

1977
———————————————————

8–29 January
Five One-Person Shows: Fritz Bultman, Gio Pomodoro, Paul Jenkins, Clayton Pond, Dennis Byng

5 February–5 March
Gershon Iskowitz
Works from the Gallery Collections: Bob Thompson, Antoni Tapies, Jean-Paul Riopelle, Joan Mitchell, James Brooks

12 March–30 April
A Salute to Carlos Merida and Francisco Toledo: Graphics (etchings and aquatints)

May
Agosti: Watercolors

Summer
Group Exhibition: Bob Thompson, James Brooks, Seymour Boardman

September 1977–March 1978
Rotating Groups Shows (works from the gallery collection)

1978

1 April–6 May
Antoni Tapies: Works 1975–77

Summer
Antoni Tapies (extended)

23 September–21 October
Elaine Kurtz: Bordered Illusions

4 November–2 December
"90 by 30:" A Festival of Small Sculpture

9 December–13 January
"Great Graphics!" (fifty graphics in all media)

1979

20 January–24 February
Julian Stanczak

3 March–14 April
Large Paintings and Small Sculpture (from the gallery's collection)

21 April–15 June
Josep Guinovart: Recent Works
Josep Royo: Tapestries
Moises Villelia: Cane Sculpture

Summer
Josep Guinovart/Josep Royo/Moises Villelia (exhibition continued)

29 September–27 October
John Hultberg and William Scott: Paintings and Drawings

3–24 November
John Griefen: New Paintings

Catalogue OF THE MARTHA JACKSON MEMORIAL COLLECTION

Artists are listed alphabetically; works are listed chronologically within each artist's entry.
Information on exhibition histories was provided by the David Anderson Gallery.

Asterisk (*) denotes works included in the NMAA exhibition

Norman Bluhm

born 28 March 1920

1. ARITIC (triptych) 1959
oil on canvas
72 x 180 in. (182.88 x 457.2 cm.)
1980.137.3
Exhibitions: Lowe Art Museum,
University of Miami, Coral Gables,
Florida, 1980

2. MATHEMATICS 1962
oil on canvas
72⅛ x 60¼ in. (182.3 x 123.0 cm.)
1980.137.2

3. MOJABE 1966
oil on canvas
90 x 72⅜ in. (228.6 x 183.8 cm.)
1980.137.7
Exhibitions: Martha Jackson Gallery,
1970, 1979

4.* ACHERON (triptych) 1971
oil on canvas
total dimensions: 66⅛ x 270¾ in.
(167.64 x 685.8 cm.)
panel dimensions: 66⅛ x 90¼ in.
(168.0 x 229.2 cm.)
1980.137.4
Exhibitions: Everson Museum of Art,
Syracuse, New York, 1973; Contemporary Arts Museum, Houston, Texas,
1976

5.* THAMYRIS 1972
oil on canvas
81¼ x 114⅜ in. (206.3 x 290.9 cm.)
1980.137.6
Exhibitions: Martha Jackson Gallery,
1974; Fort Wayne Museum of Art, Fort
Wayne, Indiana, 1976

6. DIDO 1973
oil on canvas
112 x 120 in. (284.48 x 304.8 cm.)
1980.137.5
Exhibitions: Martha Jackson Gallery,
1974; Contemporary Arts Museum,
Houston, Texas, 1976

cat. no. 7

Gandy Brody

20 May 1924–25 October 1975

7. BLACK AND WHITE DRAWING 1951
brush and ink on paper
10⅝ x 13¾ in. (27.0 x 34.9 cm.)
1980.137.8

8.* A CHIVALROUS KNIGHT 1954
watercolor, gouache, India ink, pastel,
collage on paper
18¹/₁₆ x 23¹⁵/₁₆ in. (45.9 x 60.8 cm.)
1980.137.9

James Brooks

born 18 October 1906

9.* HARMAGH 1967
acrylic on canvas
48 x 60 in. (121.92 x 152.4 cm.)
1980.137.10
Exhibitions: Martha Jackson Gallery,
1968; Dallas Museum of Fine Arts,
Dallas Texas, 1972; The Art Gallery,
University of Maryland, College Park,
Maryland, 1973; Finch College
Museum of Art, New York, New York,
1973; Albright-Knox Art Gallery, Buffalo, New York, 1974

10.* ORAN 1969
acrylic on canvas
108 x 93 in. (274.32 x 236.22 cm.)
1980.137.11
Exhibitions: Boston University Art
Gallery, Boston, Massachusetts, 1970;

Martha Jackson Gallery, 1971; Seibu
Department Store, Tokyo, Japan, 1971;
Dallas Museum of Fine Arts, Dallas,
Texas, 1972; Museum of Fine Arts, St.
Petersburg, Florida, 1973; Loch Haven
Art Center, Orlando, Florida, 1973; Le
Moyne Foundation, Tallahassee, Florida, 1973; Finch College Museum of
Art, New York, New York, 1973;
Albright-Knox Art Gallery, Buffalo,
New York, 1974; University Art
Gallery, State University of New
York, Albany, New York, 1975;
Koehler Cultural Center, San Antonio
College, San Antonio, Texas, 1975;
Miami University Art Museum,
Oxford, Ohio, 1980

Fritz Bultman

born 4 April 1919

11.* AZORES I 1959
bronze sculpture
work: 41 x 45 x 9½ in. (104.14 x 114.3 x
24.13 cm.)
stand: 30½ x 24 x 16 in. (77.47 x
60.96 x 40.64 cm.)
1980.137.15
Exhibitions: Martha Jackson Gallery,
1962, 1976

12.* THE DELTA 1959
oil on canvas
72 x 48 in. (182.88 x 121.92 cm.)
1980.137.16
Exhibitions: Martha Jackson Gallery,
1959

cat. no. 14

13.* MIKI (ORIENTAL II)   1964
pencil on paper
23⅛ x 29¹/₁₆ in. (58.6 x 73.7 cm.)
1980.137.14
Exhibitions: New Orleans Museum of
Art, New Orleans, Louisiana, 1974;
Oklahoma Art Center, Oklahoma City,
Oklahoma, 1974; Art Association of
Newport, Newport, Rhode Island, 1974

14. TACKI AND LYNN   1970
pencil on paper
23¹/₁₆ x 29¹/₁₆ in. (58.5 x 73.8 cm.)
1980.137.13
Exhibitions: New Orleans Museum of
Art, New Orleans, Louisiana, 1974;
Oklahoma Art Center, Oklahoma City,
Oklahoma, 1974; Art Association of
Newport, Newport, Rhode Island, 1974

15.* THE WAY UP AND THE WAY
    DOWN   1975
acrylic and collage on paper
90½ x 48 in. (229.87 x 121.92 cm.)
1980.137.12
Exhibitions: Martha Jackson Gallery,
1976, 1977

Dennis Byng

born 6 November 1927

16.* COLUMN WITH ORANGE, BLUE,
    GREEN DIAGONALS   1969
laminated plexiglass assemblage
18¾ x 5¾ x 6¼ in. (47.625 x 14.605 x
15.875 cm.)
1981.109.1
Exhibitions: Martha Jackson Gallery,
1969; Seibu Department Store, Tokyo,
Japan, 1971

17.* Untitled   1976
cast lucite
71 x 21 x 11¾ in. (180.34 x 53.34 x
29.845 cm.)
1981.109.2
Exhibitions: Joseloff Gallery, University of Hartford, Hartford, Connecticut,
1977; Martha Jackson Gallery, 1977

18.* 77A AA   1977
cast lucite
46¾ x 13 x 13 in. (118.745 x 33.02 x
33.02 cm.)
1981.109.3
Exhibitions: Indianapolis Museum of
Art, Indianapolis, Indiana, 1978; Worcester Art Museum, Worcester, Massachusetts, 1978

cat. no. 19

Lawrence Calcagno

born 23 March 1913

19. NIGHT TIDE, XVII   1955
oil on canvas
57¼ x 38¼ in. (145.415 x 97.155 cm.)
1981.109.4

Exhibitions: American Federation of
Arts (traveling exhibition), 1956; Finch
College Museum of Art, New York,
New York, 1973; Albright-Knox Art
Gallery, Buffalo, New York, 1974

20.* NIGHT AT MATTOON   1959
oil on canvas
47½ x 59½ in. (120.7 x 151.6 cm.)
1981.109.5

Exhibitions: Pennsylvania Academy of
the Fine Arts, Philadelphia, Pennsylvania, 1962

Dale Chisman

born 1943

21. WIRE AND STONE HEADS   1974
acrylic on canvas
71¾ x 61½ in. (182.245 x 156.21 cm.)
1980.137.17

cat. no. 21

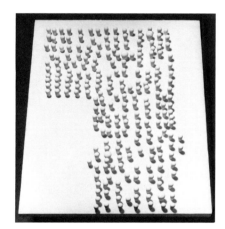

cat. no. 22

Vardea Chryssa

born 31 December 1933

22.* WHITE RELIEF   1960
gesso over plaster on wood
59¼ x 44¾ in. (150.495 x 113.665 cm.)
1980.137.18

Exhibitions: Martha Jackson Gallery,
1960; Finch College Museum of Art,
New York, New York, 1973; Albright-
Knox Art Gallery, Buffalo, New York,
1974; University Art Gallery, State
University of New York, Albany, New
York, 1975; Art Museum, Stamford,
Connecticut, 1976

cat. no. 25

Eldzier Cortor

born 10 January 1916

23.* SOUTHERN GATE   1942–43
oil on canvas
46¼ x 22 in. (117.475 x 55.88 cm.)
1980.137.19

Exhibitions: G Place Gallery, Washington, D.C., 1944; Baltimore Museum of Art, Baltimore, Maryland, 1944; City Art Museum, St. Louis, Missouri, 1944; Albany Institute of History and Art, Albany, New York, 1945–46; Albright-Knox Art Gallery, Buffalo, New York, 1945–46; Munson-Williams-Proctor Institute Museum of Art, Utica, New York, 1945–46; Museum of Art, Rhode Island School of Design, Providence, Rhode Island, 1945–46; Brooklyn Museum, Brooklyn, New York, 1945–46; Studio Museum in Harlem, New York, New York, 1969; Museum of the National Center of Afro-American Artists, Boston, Massachusetts, 1973; Studio Museum in Harlem, New York, New York, 1973

Emilio Cruz

born 15 March 1938

24.* FIGURATIVE COMPOSITION #7   1965
oil on canvas
59¼ x 67 in. (150.495 x 170.18 cm.)
1980.137.21

25. ANGOLA'S DREAMS GRASP FINGER TIPS   1973
acrylic on canvas
84 x 84 in. (213.36 x 213.36 cm.)
1980.137.20

Exhibitions: Rockland Center for the Arts, Rockland Community College, West Nyack, New York, 1974; University Art Gallery, State University of New York, Albany, New York, 1975

Jim Dine

born 16 June 1935

26.* THE VALIANT RED CAR   1960
oil on canvas
53 x 132 in. (134.62 x 335.28 cm.)
1980.137.22

Exhibitions: Martha Jackson Gallery, 1962, 1967-68; Dayton Art Institute, Dayton, Ohio, 1968; Whitney Museum of American Art, New York, New York, 1970; Rockland Center for the Arts, Rockland Community College, West Nyack, New York, 1974; University Art Gallery, State University of New York, Albany, New York, 1975

Frank Duncan

born 1916

27. RED PITCHER   1952
oil on canvas mounted on fiberboard
19¾ x 28 in. (50.165 x 71.12 cm.)
1980.137.23

Exhibitions: American Academy of Arts and Letters, New York, New York, 1959; Martha Jackson Gallery, 1977

S(tanley) D(ean) Edwards

born 5 December 1941

28. BABY IN AN ALTAR NO. IV   1964
oil and acrylic on canvas
60 x 59¾ in. (152.4 x 151.765 cm.)
1980.137.24

Marisol (Escobar)

born 22 May 1930

29.* PRESIDENT CHARLES DEGAULLE 1967
mixed media on plywood
107¼ x 86¼ x 32 in. (272.415 x 219.075 x 81.28 cm.)
1981.109.12A-E

Exhibitions: University Art Gallery, State University of New York, Albany, New York, 1975; Art Museum, Stamford, Connecticut, 1976; F.I.A.C., Paris, France, 1976

cat. no. 27

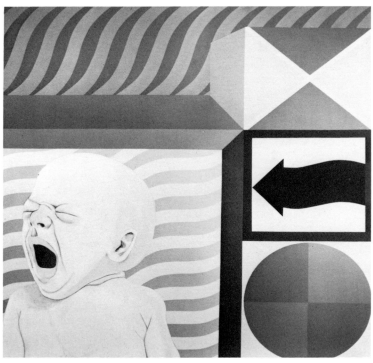

cat. no. 28

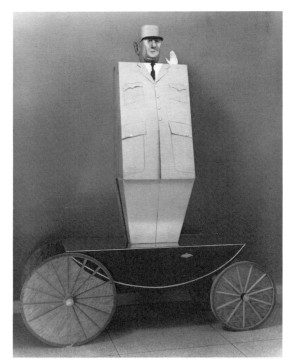

cat. no. 29

Claire Falkenstein

born 1908

30.* ENVELOPE 1958
brazed iron and fused glass, steel wire
assemblage
48 x 60 x 36 in. (121.92 x 152.4 x
91.44 cm.)
1981.109.6

Exhibitions: Martha Jackson Gallery,
1965; Seibu Department Store, Tokyo,
Japan, 1971; Katonah Gallery, Katonah,
New York, 1972; Finch College
Museum of Art, New York, New York,
1973; Albright-Knox Art Gallery, Buffalo, New York, 1974; Philadelphia
Civic Center, Philadelphia, Pennsylvania, 1974

31.* CONIC 1959
brazed copper
70 x 38½ x 10½ in. (177.8 x 97.79 x
26.67 cm.)
1981.109.7

Exhibitions: Martha Jackson Gallery,
1965; Phoenix Art Museum, Phoenix,
Arizona, 1967; Long Beach Museum of
Art, Long Beach, California, 1968

32.* CORONA 1971
brazed copper and fused glass
8¼ x 12¼ x 7½ in. (20.955 x 31.115 x
19.05 cm.)
1981.109.8

Exhibitions: Martha Jackson Gallery,
1978

Sam Francis

born 25 June 1923

33.* Untitled ca. 1948–50
oil wash on paper
21¼ x 14⅝ in. (54.0 x 37.1 cm.)
1980.137.26

Exhibitions: Albright-Knox Art Gallery,
Buffalo, New York, 1972; Maxwell
Davidson Gallery, New York, New
York, 1979; Institute of Contemporary
Art, Boston, Massachusetts, 1979

34. Untitled 1951
brush and ink and ink wash on paper
21³/₁₆ x 14⅝ in. (53.7 x 37.1 cm.)
1980.137.25

Exhibitions: Albright-Knox Art Gallery,
Buffalo, New York, 1972; Corcoran
Gallery of Art, Washington, D.C., 1972;

cat. no. 37

Whitney Museum of American Art,
New York, New York, 1973; Maxwell
Davidson Gallery, New York, New
York, 1979

35.* Untitled 1950–53
brush and ink and ink wash on paper
21¼ x 14¾ in. (23.9 x 37.4 cm.)
1980.137.27

Exhibitions: American Federation of
the Arts (traveling exhibition), 1961;

Martha Jackson Gallery, 1970;
Albright-Knox Art Gallery, Buffalo,
New York, 1972; Corcoran Gallery of
Art, Washington, D.C., 1972; Whitney
Museum of American Art, New York,
New York, 1972; Dallas Museum of
Fine Arts, Dallas, Texas, 1973; Oakland
Museum, Oakland, California, 1973;
Byron Gallery, New York, New York,
1974; Maxwell Davidson Gallery, New
York, New York, 1979; Rensselaer Poly-
technic Institute, Troy, New York, 1979

36.* BLACK RECTANGLE   1953

brush and ink and ink wash on paper
25¾ x 19¹³/₁₆ in. (65.3 x 50.2 cm.)
1980.137.29

Exhibitions: Albright-Knox Art Gallery, Buffalo, New York, 1972; Corcoran Gallery of Art, Washington, D.C., 1972; Whitney Museum of American Art, New York, New York, 1972

37.* UNTITLED #19   1959

synthetic polymer (acrylic) on paper
8 x 4¹⁵/₁₆ in. (20.4 x 12.6 cm.)
1980.137.28

Exhibitions: Sid Deutsch Gallery, New York, New York, 1977; Maxwell Davidson Gallery, New York, New York, 1979

38.* Untitled   1965

oil on canvas
90½ x 67 in. (229.87 x 170.18 cm.)
1981.109.13

David Gilhooly

born 15 April 1943

39. CEPHLAPOD 5   1971

ceramic sculpture
4¼ x 4 x 6¾ in. (10.795 x 10.16 x 17.145 cm.)
1980.137.30

Exhibitions: Martha Jackson Gallery, 1971, 1979

Michael Goldberg

born 24 December 1924

40.* SARDINES   1955

oil and adhesive tape on canvas
80¾ x 66 in. (205.105 x 167.64 cm.)
1981.109.9

Exhibitions: Rockland Center for the Arts, Rockland Community College, West Nyack, New York, 1974; University Art Gallery, State University of New York, Albany, New York, 1975; Koehler Cultural Center, San Antonio College, San Antonio, Texas, 1975; William Benton Museum of Art, University of Connecticut, Storrs, Connecticut, 1983; Newport Harbor Art Museum, Newport Beach, California, Worcester Art Museum, Worcester, Massachusetts, Grey Art Gallery, New York University, New York, New York, 1984–85

41.* THE CREEKS   1959

oil on canvas
52 x 47¾ in. (132.08 x 121.285 cm.)
1981.109.10

Exhibitions: University Gallery, University of Minnesota, Minneapolis, Minnesota, 1960

42. STILL LIFE   1965

oil on canvas
59¾ x 52 in. (151.765 x 132.08 cm.)
1981.109.11

Exhibitions: Martha Jackson Gallery, 1966

cat. no. 42

John Goodyear

born 22 October 1930

43. LANDSCAPE #2   1964

oil on wood, oil on fiberboard, four wood grids, cut and assembled
24 x 24 in. (60.96 x 60.96 cm.)
1980.137.31A-E

Exhibitions: Martha Jackson Gallery, 1965; Finch College Museum of Art, New York, New York, 1973; Albright-Knox Art Gallery, Buffalo, New York, 1974

Grace Hartigan

born 28 March 1922

44.* MODERN CYCLE   1967

oil on canvas
78 x 108¼ in. (198.12 x 274.955 cm.)
1980.137.33

Exhibitions: Pennsylvania Academy of the Fine Arts, Philadelphia, Pennsylvania, 1968; Detroit Institute of Arts, Detroit, Michigan, 1969; Krannert Art Museum, University of Illinois, Champaign, Illinois, 1969; Rockland Center for the Arts, Rockland Community College, West Nyack, New York, 1974; University Art Gallery, State University of New York, Albany, New York, 1975

cat. no. 39

45. INCLEMENT WEATHER 1970
acrylic on canvas
78¼ x 88¼ in. (198.755 x 224.155 cm.)
1980.137.32
Exhibitions: Martha Jackson Gallery,
1970

Stanley William Hayter

born 27 December 1901

46. VICTIME 1946
oil on canvas
36 x 60 in. (91.44 x 152.4 cm.)
1980.137.34
Exhibitions: Fine Arts Center, Colorado
Springs, Colorado, 1950

cat. no. 45

cat. no. 46

92

cat. no. 47

John Hultberg

born 8 February 1922

47. BLACK AND WHITE   1952
oil on canvas
46½ x 52 in. (118.11 x 132.08 cm.)
1980.137.62

48. AFTER DE CHIRICO   1953
oil on canvas
37⅞ x 48⅞ in. (96.3 x 124.2 cm.)
1980.137.57

49.* IMAGINARY LANDSCAPE   1954
ink and conté crayon on paper
18¹¹/₁₆ x 19³/₁₆ in. (46.355 x 41.91 cm.)
1980.137.61
Exhibitions: Brooklyn Museum, Brooklyn, New York, 1956-57

cat. no. 48

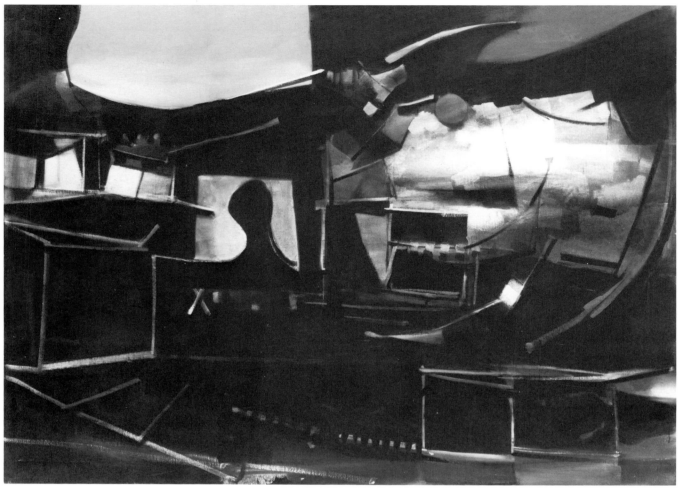

cat. no. 50

50. BLUE 1955
oil on canvas
40 x 54 in. (101.6 x 137.16 cm.)
1980.137.63

51. WHITE PERSPECTIVE 1956
oil on canvas
48 x 72 in. (121.92 x 182.9 cm.)
1980.137.56

Exhibitions: Hultberg Western Travel
Show, 1960–61; Martha Jackson
Gallery, 1964; Westchester Art Society,
1965; Museum of Fine Arts, St. Petersburg, Florida, 1970

52.* MACHINE SHOP (Showing Gantry
      Cranes, Newport News Shipyard)
      1957

gouache, charcoal, pencil, and crayon
on paperboard (Whatman Drawing
Board)
21^{15}/$_{16}$1980.137.59

cat. no. 51

53.* NEW CITY   1957

oil on canvas
50⅞ x 76⅝ in. (129.3 x 194.6 cm.)
1980.137.58

Exhibitions: Hultberg Western Travel
Show, 1960–61; Martha Jackson
Gallery, 1972

54.* THE BLACK FLAG   1957

oil on canvas
32 x 42 in. (81.28 x 106.68 cm.)
1980.137.60

Exhibitions: University of Mississippi,
University, Mississippi, 1958;
Washington University Gallery of Art,
St. Louis, Missouri, 1958; Flint Institute
of Arts, Flint, Michigan, 1959

55.* BLUE BLACK DESTRUCTION   1958

oil on canvas
50 x 72¾ in. (127.0 x 182.3 cm.)
1980.137.55

Exhibitions: American Swedish
Museum, Philadelphia, Pennsylvania,
1959; Martha Jackson Gallery, 1959;
Indiana University Art Center Gallery,
Bloomington, Indiana, 1959; Corcoran
Gallery of Art, Washington, D.C., 1961;
USIA Traveling Show, Paris, France,
1969

56. CONTROL TOWER   1959

oil on canvas
40 x 50⅛ in. (101.6 x 127.3 cm.)
1980.137.54

Exhibitions: Gallery of Modern Art,
Scottsdale, Arizona, 1966-67

57. GREY SPACE FORMS   1959

oil on canvas
32 x 40 in. (81.28 x 101.6 cm.)
1980.137.53

Exhibitions: Martha Jackson Gallery,
1959

cat. no. 56

cat. no. 57

cat. no. 58

58. INTERIOR   1959
oil on board
24 x 30 in. (60.96 x 76.2 cm.)
1980.137.52

Exhibitions: Hultberg Western Travel
Show, 1960–61

59. MONHEGAN DOCK   1961
oil on canvas board
20 x 24 in. (50.8 x 60.96 cm.)
1980.137.42

60. PLAIN WITH FLAG   1961
gouache on board
22 x 30 in. (55.88 x 76.2 cm.)
1980.137.51

cat. no. 59

cat. no. 61

cat. no. 63

61. SURF INVASION   1962
oil on canvas
50 x 68 in. (127.0 x 172.72 cm.)
1980.137.50
Exhibitions: University of Arizona,
Museum of Art, Tucson, Arizona,
1964-65

62.* GIANT   1963
oil on canvas
84¾ x 119¼ in. (212.7 x 402.9 cm.)
1980.137.47
Exhibitions: Martha Jackson Gallery,
1969, 1972; The Art Gallery, University
of Maryland, College Park, Maryland,
1972–73; Finch College Museum of Art,
New York, New York, 1973; Albright-
Knox Art Gallery, Buffalo, New York,
1974

63. DEMON CLOUD   1963
oil on canvas
34⅛ x 40¼ in. (87.2 x 102.23 cm.)
1980.137.49

97

64. THE GENERAL   1966
oil on canvas
40 x 32 in. (101.6 x 81.28 cm.)
1980.137.48
Exhibitions: Martha Jackson Gallery, 1966; University of Arizona Museum of Art, Tucson, Arizona, 1966–67; Spectrum Gallery, New York, New York, 1967

65. SCULPTOR'S GARDEN   1968
oil on canvas
50⅛ x 68 in. (127.3 x 172.72 cm.)
1980.137.46

66. Untitled   1968
gouache on board
24 x 30 in. (60.96 x 76.2 cm.)
1980.137.45

67. DREDGINGS   1969
oil on canvas
50⅛ x 68 in. (127.2 x 172.72 cm.)
1980.137.43
Exhibitions: Martha Jackson Gallery, 1970

68. SQUALL   1969
gouache on board
22 x 30 in. (55.88 x 76.2 cm.)
1980.137.41

69. WHITE MORNING SKY   1969
oil on board
30 x 40 in. (76.2 x 101.6 cm.)
1980.137.44
Exhibitions: Lehigh University Art Galleries, Bethlehem, Pennsylvania, 1972; N.S.C.G.C., Manhasset, New York, 1973

70. LEAVING THE WORLD'S ROOM   1972
oil on canvas
29¾ x 40⅛ in. (75.6 x 102.0 cm.)
1980.137.36

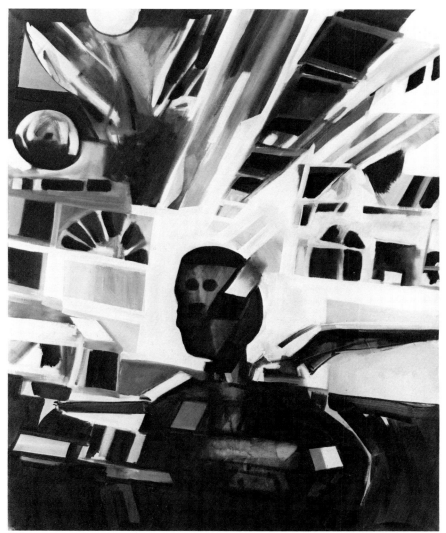

cat. no. 64

cat. no. 65

98

cat. no. 67

cat. no. 70

cat. no. 71

71. FUTURE ARCHEOLOGY 1972
oil on canvas
50¼ x 68¼ in. (127.6 x 173.3 cm.)
1980.137.40
Exhibitions: Martha Jackson Gallery,
1974

72. ORDERLY EXPLOSION 1973
ink and gouache on board
20 x 30 in. (50.8 x 76.2 cm.)
1980.137.39

73.* UNDER RED GLASS 1974
brush and ink and gouache on colored
paper mounted on paperboard
29¼ x 45¹³/₁₆ in. (74.2 x 116.3 cm.)
1980.137.38

cat no. 74

cat. no. 75

74. DESECRATION OF THE HOUSE   1977
acrylic and oil on canvas
48 x 60 in. (121.92 x 152.4 cm.)
1980.137.37
Exhibitions: American Academy and
Institute of Arts and Letters, New York,
New York, 1978

75. ROAD THROUGH THE LABYRINTH
    1979
oil on canvas
48 x 65 in. (121.92 x 165.1 cm.)
1980.137.35
Exhibitions: Martha Jackson Gallery,
1979

Lester Johnson

born 27 January 1919

76.* TWO HEADS: RED   1961
oil on canvas
48 x 60 in. (121.92 x 152.4 cm.)
1980.137.71
Exhibitions: Martha Jackson Gallery,
1979

77.* BROADWAY STREET SCENE   1962
oil on canvas
60¼ x 78¼ in. (153.0 x 198.7 cm.)
1980.137.70
Exhibitions: Martha Jackson Gallery,
1963; Lawrence University, Appleton,
Wisconsin, 1968; Herbert F. Johnson
Museum of Art, Cornell University,
Ithaca, New York, 1968; Bowdoin Col-
lege, Museum of Art, Brunswick,
Maine, 1968; College of Wooster Art
Museum, Wooster, Ohio, 1968;
Bloomsburg University, Bloomsburg,

Pennsylvania, 1968; Municipal Univer-
sity of Omaha, Omaha, Nebraska, 1968;
The Art Gallery, University of Mary-
land, College Park, Maryland, 1973;
Finch College Museum of Art, New
York, New York, 1973; Albright-Knox
Art Gallery, Buffalo, New York, 1974;
Rockland Center for the Arts, Rock-
land Community College, West Nyack,
New York, 1974; University Art
Gallery, State University of New York,
Albany, New York, 1975; Koehler Cul-
tural Center, San Antonio College, San
Antonio, Texas, 1975

cat. no. 78

78. WALKING MEN GREEN 1963
oil on canvas
80¼ x 59⅝ in. (204.0 x 151.5 cm.)
1980.137.69

Exhibitions: New School for Social
Research, New York, New York, 1964;
Yale University Art Gallery, New
Haven, Connecticut, 1965

79.* BEETHOVEN WITH STOVE 1964
oil on canvas
68 x 50¼ in. (172.72 x 127.3 cm.)
1980.137.68

Exhibitions: Martha Jackson Gallery,
1965

80.* TWO SELF PORTRAITS 1965
oil on canvas
80 x 60 in. (203.2 x 152.4 cm.)
1980.137.67

Exhibitions: Smithsonian Institution,
Washington, D.C., 1970

cat. no. 82

81.* THREE GRACES BLUE   1966

oil on canvas
66 x 70 in. (167.64 x 177.165 cm.)
1980.137.66

Exhibitions: Whitney Museum of
American Art, New York, New York,
1967–68

82. FIVE MEN WITH HATS   1968

oil on canvas
68⅛ x 74¾ in. (173.0 x 187.4 cm.)
1980.137.65

Exhibitions: Martha Jackson Gallery,
1969, 1979; Madrid, Spain, 1969;
Temple University, Tyler School of Art,
Philadelphia, Pennsylvania, 1974; Jor-
enson Art Center, University of Con-
necticut, Storrs, Connecticut, 1975;
Livingston-Learmonth Gallery, New
York, New York, 1975

83.* CITY WOMEN   1973

oil on canvas
39⅞ x 50 in. (101.5 x 127.0 cm.)
1980.137.64

Exhibitions: National Academy of
Design, New York, New York, 1974;
Temple University, Tyler School of Art,
Philadelphia, Pennsylvania, 1974; Jor-
enson Art Center, University of Con-
necticut, Storrs, Connecticut, 1975

cat. no. 89

Alex Katz

born 24 July 1927

Catalogue numbers 84–94 are eleven of the twenty cutout figures and props that Katz designed for Kenneth Koch's GEORGE WASHINGTON CROSSING THE DELAWARE. The exhibition history for the eleven pieces is listed once.

Exhibitions: Martha Jackson Gallery, 1962; Finch College Museum of Art, New York, New York, 1973; The Art Gallery, University of Maryland, College Park, Maryland, 1973; Albright-Knox Art Gallery, Buffalo, New York, 1974; New Jersey State Museum, Trenton, New Jersey, 1975; Mary and Leigh Block Gallery, Northwestern University, Evanston, Illinois, 1980

84.* JAPAN CHINA TEAPOT   1961
china
7 x 7 x 5 in. (17.78 x 17.78 x 12.7 cm.)
1980.137.74

85.* LANTERN   1961
acrylic on plywood
15 x 7¼ x ¼ in. (38.1 x 18.415 x .635 cm.)
1980.137.72

86.* TABLE AND CAKE   1961
acrylic on wood
38 x 26 x 15 in. (96.52 x 66.04 x 8.1 cm.)
1980.137.73

87.* WHITE HORSE   1961
oil on wood cutout
89½ x 96¾ x 26 in. (227.33 x 245.754 x 66.04 cm.)
1979.56.1

88.* AMERICAN REVOLUTIONARY SOLDIER   1961
oil on plywood cutout
56 x 17½ x 6⅓ in. (142.24 x 44.45 x 16.129 cm.)
1980.139.1. Gift of Aaron Kozac.

89.* AMERICAN FLAG AND SOLDIERS 1961
oil on wood cutout
79½ x 103½ x 18½ in. (201.93 x 262.89 x 46.99 cm.)
1979.56.2A

90.* RIVER   1961
oil on wood cutout
15¾ x 219¾ x 1 in. (40.005 x 558.165 x 2.54 cm.)
1979.56.2B

91.* SIGN: THE DREAM OF GEORGE WASHINGTON   1961
oil on wood cutout
75 x 36 in. (190.5 x 91.44 cm.)
1979.56.2C

92.* BRITISH SOLDIERS (set of three) 1961
acrylic on wood
66 x 24.25 x 6.5 in., 66.25 x 24.25 x 6.5 in., 66.75 x 24.25 x 6.5 in. (167.64 x 61.595 x 16.51 cm., 168.275 x 61.595 x 16.51 cm., x 169.545 x 16.51 cm.)
1980.137.75A-C

93.* AMERICAN REVOLUTIONARY SOLDIER   1961
oil on plywood cutout
60¾ x 19 x 6⅓ in. (154.305 x 48.26 x 16.129 cm.)
1980.139.2. Gift of Aaron Kozac.

94.* TWO TEA CUPS   1961
polychrome on wood
4⅞ x 7⅜ x 3 in., 5⅛ x 7⅝ x 3 in. (12.4 x 18.7 x 7.6 cm., 13.0 x 19.4 x 7.6 cm.)
1980.137.105, 1980.137.106

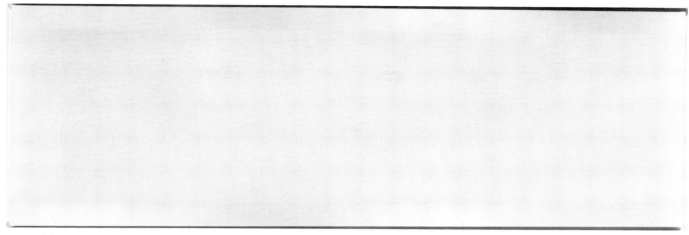

cat. no. 96

Elaine Kurtz

born 1928

95.* UNTITLED (WHITE)   1980
acrylic on canvas
overall: 124½ x 33 in. (311.0 x
83.9 cm.)
two panels: 120 x 15 in. (304.9 x 38.2)
1980.137.1

96. WHITE SPECTRUM   1982
acrylic on canvas
42½ x 122½ in. (107.95 x 311.15 cm.)
1982.76. Gift of Elaine Kurtz.

Frank Lobdell

born 1921

97.* DECEMBER 1958   1958
oil on canvas
69¼ x 58 in. (175.895 x 147.32 cm.)
1980.137.76

Exhibitions: M. H. de Young Memorial
Museum, San Francisco, California,
1960; Martha Jackson Gallery, 1960;
Stanford University Museum and Art
Gallery, Stanford, California, 1966; Pasadena Art Museum, Pasadena, California, 1966

98.* SUMMER 1962   1962
oil on canvas
69¾ x 97¼ in. (177.165 x 247.015 cm.)
1980.137.77

Exhibitions: Stanford University
Museum and Art Gallery, Stanford,
California, 1966; Pasadena Art
Museum, Pasadena, California, 1966;
Martha Jackson Gallery, 1974

Ed McGowin

born 2 June 1938

99. UNTITLED (ARCHES)   1966
vacuum formed plastic relief
32¾ x 29½ x 6 in. (83.185 x 73.66 x
15.24 cm.)
1980.137.80

cat. no. 99

100.* THREE LOCKED PYRAMIDS   1967
charcoal and pencil on paper
24¹/₁₆ x 36¹/₁₆ in. (61.0 x 91.5 cm.)
1980.137.78

101. UNTITLED RELIEF   1968
vacuum formed plastic relief
15½ x 51½ x 2¾ in. (39.37 x 130.8 x
6.985 cm.)
1980.137.79

Exhibitions: Riverside Museum, New
York, New York, 1968

cat. no. 101

cat. no. 106

Joan Mitchell

born 12 February 1926

102.* MY LANDSCAPE II 1967
oil on canvas
103 x 71½ in. (261.62 x 181.61 cm.)
1980.137.82
Exhibitions: Martha Jackson Gallery,
1969, 1979; Virginia Museum of Arts,
Richmond, Virginia, 1970; Everson
Museum of Art, Syracuse, New York,
1972

103.* SUNFLOWER III 1969
oil on canvas
112½ x 78½ in. (285.75 x 199.39 cm.)
1980.137.81
Exhibitions: Seibu Department Store,
Tokyo, Japan, 1971; Everson Museum of
Art, Syracuse, New York, 1972;
Washington County Museum, 1979

Louise Nevelson

born 23 September 1899

104.* WORLD GARDEN CABINET 1959
wood painted black
57 x 11½ x 10½ in. (144.78 x 29.21 x
26.67 cm.)
1980.137.83
Exhibitions: C. W. Post College, Green-
vale, New York, 1974

105.* GATE V (GARDEN GATE SERIES)
1959-60
cast bronze 3/3
46 x 31½ x 2⅓ in. (116.84 x 80.01 x
5.969 cm.)
1980.137.84
Exhibitions: Martha Jackson Gallery,
1963; Rockland Community College,
Suffern, New York, 1974

Phillip Pavia

born 15 March 1913

106.* AMAZON ON HORSEBACK 1966
Greek marble
35 in. (88.9 cm.) high
1980.137.86
Exhibitions: Martha Jackson Gallery,
1966; Wilmington Society of Fine Arts,
1967; Walker Art Center, Minneapolis,
Minnesota, 1974-76

107.* PORTRAIT HEAD OF MARTHA
JACKSON 1971
cast bronze
11¾ x 6 x 8 in. (29.845 x 15.24 x
20.32 cm.)
1980.137.85

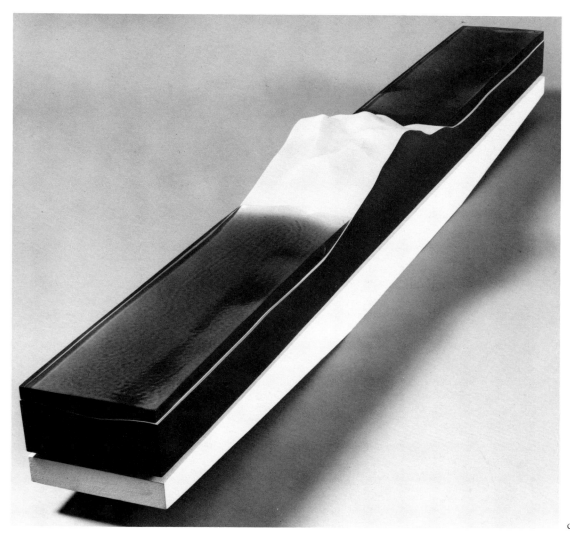

Sam Richardson

born 19 July 1934

108.* A Very Thick Summer Overcast
    Extending Inland Near Antioch,
    California   1969

polyurethane foam, resin, acrylic, and
Lacquer
work: 53 x 62 x 14 in. (134.62 x 157.48 x
35.56 cm.)
base: 30½ x 60 x 5 in. (77.47 x 152.4 x
12.7 cm.)
1980.137.87

Exhibitions: Martha Jackson Gallery,
1969; Center for the Fine Arts, Miami,
Florida, 1970; Museum of Fine Arts, St.
Petersburg, Florida, 1970; Mills College
Art Gallery, Oakland, California, 1973;
Cranbrook Academy of Art Museum,
Bloomfield Hills, Michigan, 1973; The
Art Gallery, University of Maryland,
College Park, Maryland, 1973; Finch
College Museum of Art, New York,
New York, 1973; Albright-Knox Art
Gallery, Buffalo, New York, 1974

109.* It's a Cool October Evening
    with a Little Lake at the Base
    of that Hill   1969

polyurethane foam, resin, acrylic, and
Lacquer
work: 56 x 5 x 5 in. (142.24 x 12.7 x 12.7
cm.)
base: ¼ x 12 x 12 in. (.635 x 30.48 x
30.48 cm.)
1980.137.88

Exhibitions: Martha Jackson Gallery,
1969, 1978; The Art Gallery, University
of Maryland, College Park, Maryland,
1973; Albright-Knox Art Gallery, Buffalo, New York, 1974

110. It's Getting Darker on the East
    Side of that Island because the
    Sun is Setting in the West   1970

polyurethane foam, resin, acrylics, lacquers, and wood
work: 6½ x 69½ x 7¼ in. (16.5 x
176.5 x 18.4 cm.)
base: 4 x 69½ x 7¼ in. (10.2 x
176.5 x 18.4 cm.)
sub-base: 26 x 21½ x 7¼ in. (66 x 54.6 x
18.4 cm.)
1980.137.90

Exhibitions: Martha Jackson Gallery,
1970; Rockland Community College,
Suffern, New York, 1972

111. It Is Summer and the Tree Waits
    on Top of that Hill   1972

polyurethane foam, resin, acrylic, and
Lacquer (plexiglass)
35 x 84 x 6 in. (88.9 x 213.36 x 24 cm.)
1980.137.89

Exhibitions: Akron Art Institute,
Akron, Ohio, 1972; Martha Jackson
Gallery, 1972; State University of New
York, Potsdam, New York, 1975

112.* Sierra Snow: Sunrise on East
    Face   1974

polyurethane, plexiglass, and wood
9 x 16 x 16 in. (22.86 x 40.64 x 40.64
cm.)
1980.137.91

Exhibitions: Martha Jackson Gallery,
1975

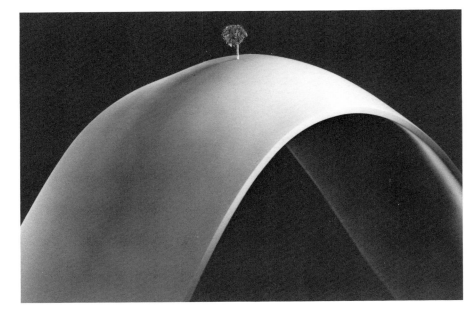

cat. no. 111

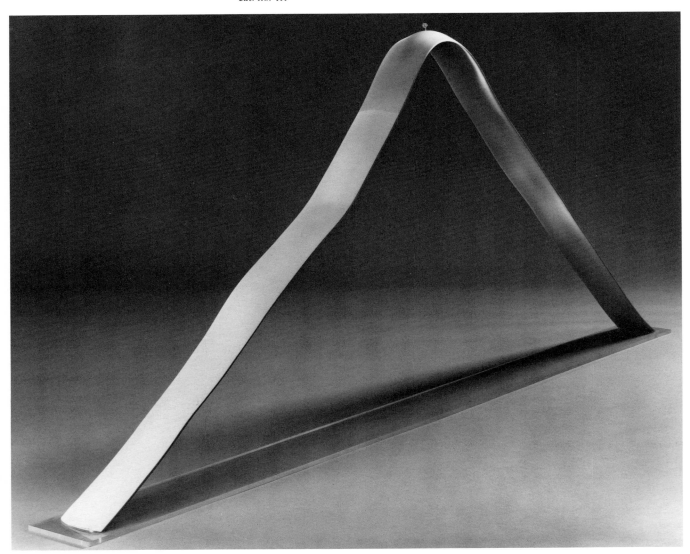

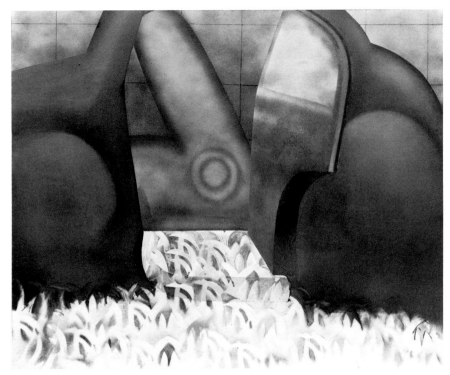

cat. no. 113

John Salt

born 1937

113. INGRESS II   1968
oil on canvas
60⅛ x 69¾ in. (152.7 x 177.2 cm.)
1980.137.92
Exhibitions: Delaware Art Center,
Wilmington, Delaware, 1969

Thomas J. Scott

ca. 1830–March 1898

114. PORTRAIT OF LEXINGTON
    ca. 1857–59

oil on canvas mounted on masonite
24¼ x 34¼ in. (61.595 x 86.995 cm.)
1980.137.93

cat. no. 114

cat. no. 118

Jochen Seidel

1 April 1924–30 May 1971

115.* MIND YOUR TRAIN DEPOSITORY
   ca.1963–67
pastel on paper
35¹/₁₆ x 22⅝ in. (89.0 x 57.4 cm.)
1980.137.95

116.* TRAIN YOUR MIND   1963–67
pastel on paper
35¹/₁₆ x 22⅝ in. (89.0 x 57.4 cm.)
1980.137.94

Exhibitions: Martha Jackson Gallery,
1976

Julian Stanczak

born 5 November 1928

117.* DETERMINATIVE FOCUS   1962
polymer and tempera on canvas
35½ x 45½ in. (90.17 x 115.57 cm.)
1980.137.96

Exhibitions: Martha Jackson Gallery,
1964, 1979; The Art Gallery, University
of Maryland, College Park, Maryland,
1973; Finch College Museum of Art,
New York, New York, 1973; Albright-
Knox Art Gallery, Buffalo, New York,
1974

118. CONDUCIVE TO YELLOW   1967
acrylic on canvas, synthetic polymer
52 x 52 in. (132.08 x 132.08 cm.)
1980.137.97
Exhibitions: Martha Jackson Gallery,
1978

119. FOUR COOLS   1969
acrylic on canvas, synthetic polymer
48 x 48 in. (121.92 x 121.92 cm.)
1980.137.98

120.* RECTANGULAR FOLD IN
        YELLOW   1971
acrylic on canvas
52 x 130 in. (132.08 x 330.2 cm.)
1980.137.99

121. SUSPENDED IN GRAYS   1975
acrylic on canvas
70 x 94 in. (177.8 x 238.76 cm.)
1980.137.101
Exhibitions: Martha Jackson Gallery,
1979

cat. no. 119

cat. no. 121

cat. no. 122

122. TRANSLUCENT   1975
acrylic on canvas
80 x 70 in. (203.2 x 177.8 cm.)
1980.137.100

Exhibitions: Martha Jackson Gallery,
1975

123.* MAJESTIC   1978
(2 canvases, red and blue)
acrylic on canvas
70 x 40 in., 70 x 70 in. (177.8 x
101.6 cm., 177.8 x 177.8 cm.)
1980.137.102A, B.

Exhibitions: Martha Jackson Gallery,
1979

Bob Thompson

26 June 1937–30 May 1966

124.* ENCHANTED RIDER   1961
oil on canvas
62¾ x 46⅞ in. (159.385 x 119.126 cm.)
1975.21

Exhibitions: New School for Social
Research, New York, New York, 1968;
National Collection of Fine Arts (now
National Museum of American Art),
Smithsonian Institution, Washington,
D.C., 1976

125.* THE SPINNING, SPINNING, TURNING,
DIRECTING   1963
oil on canvas
63 x 86½ in. (160.02 x 219.71 cm.)
1980.137.104

Exhibitions: Martha Jackson Gallery,
1968, 1972, 1976, 1979; The New
School for Social Research, New York,
New York, 1969; Roth Museum,
Geneva, Switzerland, 1971; University
Art Gallery, University of Massachu-
setts, Amherst, Massachusetts, 1974;
National Collection of Fine Arts (now
NMAA), Smithsonian Institution,
Washington, D.C., 1976; Everson
Museum of Art, Syracuse, New York,
1977; Provincetown Art Association,
Provincetown, Massachusetts, 1977;
The Studio Museum in Harlem, New
York, New York, 1979

126.* DESCENT FROM THE CROSS   1963
oil on canvas
84 x 60⅛ in. (213.4 x 152.4 cm.)
1977.16

Exhibitions: New School for Social
Research, New York, New York, 1969;
University Art Gallery, University of
Massachusetts, Amherst, Massachu-
setts, 1974; National Collection of Fine
Arts (now NMAA), Smithsonian Insti-
tution, Washington, D.C., 1975–76;
National Museum of American Art,
Smithsonian Institution, Washington,
D.C., 1982

127.* PRAYERS IN A LANDSCAPE (from
Piero della Francesca's *The Legend
of the Cross: Hercules Bringing the
Cross to Jerusalem*)   1966
crayon on paper mounted on canvas
56 x 71¾ in. (142.24 x 182.245 cm.)
1980.137.103

Exhibitions: Martha Jackson Gallery,
1968,1972; New School for Social
Research, New York, New York, 1969;
University Art Gallery, University of
Massachusetts, Amherst, Massachu-
setts, 1974

cat. no. 124

Design by Gerard Valerio, Bookmark Studio, Annapolis, Maryland

Typeset in Trump Mediaeval by Brown Composition, Inc., Baltimore, Maryland

Printed by Schneidereith & Sons, Baltimore, Maryland